The $100,000+ Entrepreneur
How to Build a Successful New Business in 90 Days

Also by Wendy S. Enelow

100 Winning Resumes for $100,000+ Jobs
201 Winning Cover Letters for $100,000+ Jobs
1500+ KeyWords for $100,000+ Jobs
The $100,000+ Entrepreneur
The $100,000+ Job Interview
Best Career Transition Resumes for $100,000+ Jobs
Best Cover Letters for $100,000+ Jobs
Best Keywords for Resumes, Cover Letters, and Interviews
Best Resumes and CVs for International Jobs
Best Resumes and Letters for Ex-Offenders
Best Resumes for $100,000+ Jobs
Best Resumes for People Without a Four-Year Degree
College Grad Resumes to Land $75,000+ Jobs
Cover Letter Magic
Executive Job Search for $100,000+ to $1 Million+ Jobs
Expert Resumes for Baby Boomers
Expert Resumes for Career Changers
Expert Resumes for Computer & Web Jobs
Expert Resumes for Health Care Careers
Expert Resumes for Managers & Executives
Expert Resumes for Manufacturing Careers
Expert Resumes for Military-to-Civilian Transitions
Expert Resumes for People Returning to Work
Expert Resumes for Teachers & Educators
Insider's Guide to Finding a Job
Keywords to Nail Your Job Interview
Million Dollar Career Tips
No-Nonsense Cover Letters
No-Nonsense Resumes

The
$100,000+
Entrepreneur

How to Build a Successful New Business in 90 Days

**Wendy S. Enelow,
CCM, MRW, JCTC, CPRW**

IMPACT PUBLICATIONS
Manassas Park, VA

The $100,000+ Entrepreneur

Library of Congress: 2006932230

ISBN: 978-1-57023-257-2 (13-digit); 1-57023-257-1 (10-digit)

Publisher: For information on Impact Publications, including current and forthcoming publications, authors, press kits, online bookstore, and submission requirements, visit Impact's website: www.impactpublications.com.

Publicity/Rights: For information on publicity, author interviews, and subsidiary rights, contact the Public Relations Department, Tel. 703-361-7300, Fax 703-335-9486, or email: query@impactpublications.com.

Sales/Distribution: All bookstore sales are handled through Impact's trade distributor, National Book Network, 15200 NBN Way, Blue Ridge Summit, PA, 17214, Tel. 1-800-462-6420. All other sales and distribution inquiries should be directed to the publisher: IMPACT PUBLICATIONS, 9104 Manassas Drive, Suite N, Manassas Park, VA 20111-5211, Tel. 703-361-7300, Fax 703-335-9486, or email: query@impactpublications.com.

Contents

Preface vii

1 Welcome to the World of Entrepreneurship 1

2 Position Yourself for Entrepreneurial Success 7

3 Even Columbus Needed a Map 28

4 Building Your Empire:
     Sales, Marketing, Branding, Advertising, and More 57

5 Customers, Clients, and Patrons:
     Can't Live With Them; Can't Live Without Them! 85

6 Money: *Does It Grow on Your Tree?* 110

7 One Day at a Time:
     Managing Your Daily Business Operations 134

8 Technology: *It's a Tool, Not a Solution* 146

9 How Well Do You Juggle?
     Managing Your Time and Productivity 167

10 Soaring High:
      Secrets to Long-Term Entrepreneurial Success 184

Subject Index 206
Resource Index 209
Entrepreneurship and Career Resources 210

Preface

TWENTY-EIGHT YEARS AND four businesses later, I've learned some hard lessons and taken some hard knocks. Most important of all, I've discovered what it takes to be a successful entrepreneur.

Early on in my entrepreneurial career, I made some terrible decisions, invested in dreadful marketing and business-building activities, hired the wrong people, was unclear about my market focus, and made just about every mistake that new entrepreneurs make. Now, all of these years later, I've learned to do it right and do it well! Those are the lessons, strategies, techniques, and tactics that I share with you in this book.

I've had a great entrepreneurial career! I started my first business, Computer Creations, at age 22 in Catonsville, Maryland. That was in the early 1970s when the first-ever word processors hit the market. I word processed documents, edited doctoral dissertations, and dabbled in resume writing.

A few years later, Computer Creations was acquired by a well-established resume-writing firm and I started writing resumes on a full-time basis. Two years later, I launched The Advantage Executive Coaching & Resume Writing Center, a company I operated for 15 years. I then sold that and started the Career Masters Institute, a training and networking association for professionals in the careers industry (e.g., resume writers, career coaches and counselors, outplacement consultants). Of course, five years later, I was bored (the entrepreneur's disease!), so I sold that. Today, I own and operate Enelow Enterprises, Inc., the corporate umbrella for everything that I do—executive coaching and career consulting, resume writing, public speaking, books, and much more.

Being an entrepreneur is great! I would never consider doing anything else. In fact, I have been offered several great "jobs" over the years, but am not the least bit interested. I like controlling my own destiny, making all of the important decisions, defining my work schedule, and being totally responsible for what happens in my business. And, if you're reading this book, you will too!

The $100,000+ Entrepreneur will tell you what no one ever tells you—the truth about entrepreneurship—the plusses, the minuses, and the multiple responsibilities. Entrepreneurship is not easy. It's demanding, it can be frustrating, you will definitely have times when you feel overwhelmed, and you must be willing to work extremely hard to achieve your goals. However, when you succeed, the personal and professional rewards can be amazing!

Be certain to have realistic expectations. There are very few of us who will rise to the level of entrepreneurial success as have Bill Gates of Microsoft, Jeff Bezos of Amazon, Oprah, and others. Most of us will be successful small-business owners who love what we do, find tremendous self-satisfaction in our businesses, and make a good living.

Opportunities for entrepreneurs are abundant in today's economy thanks to the Internet and so many other changes. As businesses have downsized, rightsized, been acquired, merged, and/or reinvented themselves over the past 20 years, entrepreneurship has exploded. Why let your professional career be at the whimsy of a large corporation when it can be under your control? Think of the potential that exists for you to reap all of the professional, financial, and personal benefits of working for yourself!

The $100,000+ Entrepreneur eliminates the mysteries of starting your own business and gives you a 90-day action plan to guide you in developing your own successful company. This practical book leads you through the entire process of new business start-up with key chapters on Business Development, Sales and Marketing, Client Relationship Management, Budgeting and Finance, Technology, Franchising, Time Management and Productivity, People Management, and much more. How you proceed over those 90 days will vary based on the type of company you are starting. However, most of everything outlined in this book should be addressed prior to launching of your new venture.

If you're at a crossroads in your career, ready to take control of your life, and committed to your new business, *The $100,000+ Entrepreneur* will help you make critical decisions for ensuring your entrepreneurial success.

1 Welcome to the World of Entrepreneurship

ENTREPRENEURSHIP IS HOT! Indeed, the 2006 Yahoo Small Business and Harris Interactive survey found that 66% of respondents wanted to own their own business; 37% indicated they desired to do so within five years. Each semester, college students flock to overflowing entrepreneurial courses in the hope of learning the inside secrets of becoming a successful entrepreneur. As *Fortune Small Business* (February 2007) notes, "We are in the midst of the largest entrepreneurial surge this country has ever seen." In fact, according to the Small Business Administration, nearly 672,000 businesses were started in 2005—the largest number ever—and the numbers are expected to increase annually by more than 10% throughout the foreseeable future. From teenagers to retirees, the desire to own and operate a business is a dream of millions of Americans and recently arrived immigrants.

The U.S. has nearly 26 million businesses, of which 20 million are sole proprietorships. Approximately 99% of those 20 million businesses have fewer than 500 employees. More so than any other country in the world, the U.S. is the home of the entrepreneur, as well as home to a disproportionate number of get-rich-quick dreamers who yearn to make six- and seven-figure incomes a year. Dreams do come true for those who become entrepreneur savvy—something you will become as you put this book into practice.

Benefits and Myths

Entrepreneurship can offer you a career and a lifestyle that can't be beat! Just think of all the benefits that entrepreneurship can bring to you:

- Higher salary or earnings
- Financial freedom
- Flexibility
- Self-prescribed workday
- Independence

- Ownership
- Sense of purpose
- Respectability
- Pride
- Self-made lifestyle

Yet, each of these benefits comes with a price! While many fledgling entrepreneurs have grandiose visions of becoming an overnight success—making $100,000 within the first year—few ever do. Indeed, the greatest misconceptions about self-employment are that you can work whenever you want, take time off whenever you want, set up the perfect work schedule that will accommodate you and your family, have lots of excess cash, and more. The reality is often quite different: As an entrepreneur you get to **choose** which 16 hours a day you would like to work!

The Challenges

Most people find few challenges riskier and more time-consuming than starting their own businesses. Self-employment generally does not offer you a lifestyle of luxury and ease, along with a happy-go-lucky attitude. You may not get a paycheck every two weeks, and occasionally you may not get paid at all. Furthermore, you may work 12-, 14-, or 16-hour days, seven days a week, and have no vacation for the first several years. What profits you do realize will most likely be poured back into the business and you may find yourself in debt, experience frequent cash-flow problems, and eventually have creditors descend on you. The stress can be enormous, so you must realize that owning a business is a 24/7 responsibility that you have to be willing to accept and commit to.

Owning a business is a 24/7 responsibility that you must accept and commit to.

If you decide to go into business for yourself, be sure you know what you want to do, and be willing to take risks and work hard. Don't expect to get rich overnight or sit back and watch your business grow on its own. Starting a business is usually a very sobering experience that tests your motivations, skills, and abilities. Success in a corporate or bureaucratic career may not transfer well to starting your own business, which initially requires a great deal of financial risk-taking and a steadfast entrepreneurial spirit and drive. Be prepared to work long and hard hours, experience disappointments, and challenge yourself to the limits. You will quickly discover this is the old-fashioned way of making money—hard work, long hours, and an unrelenting commitment to success.

What's more, business is often a trial-and-error process in which it is difficult to predict or ensure outcomes. Despite the fact that you work hard and make intelligent decisions, there are often unforeseen circumstances beyond your control, from illness to a downturn in the economy, that can negatively impact your business and your finances. Consider, for example, the tens of thousands of dot-com companies that sprang up in the late 1990s—many of which were small entrepreneurial ventures—and what happened to them when the dot-com bubble burst. Thousands went bankrupt and their owners found themselves out of work and out of money.

The Rewards

Yet, owning a business can be tremendously satisfying. Being your own boss means you have total control. What happens in your business and your career is entirely dependent on you and your own successes and failures. You are rewarded, professionally and financially, in direct proportion to your productivity and your expertise. Your salary is not limited by your boss, nor are your accomplishments credited to others. Unless you decide otherwise, you are not wedded to a 9-to-5 work routine or a two-week vacation each year. Depending on how successful your business becomes, you may earn significant financial returns and be able to retire at a much earlier age than most of your peers.

It's for these reasons, and many others, that more and more individuals are launching their own entrepreneurial ventures and taking advantage of the entrepreneurial lifestyle. In fact, if you talk to people who have worked for others and then started their own businesses, they will often tell you similar stories, which include both positive and negative reasons, for making a career change and leaving the traditional workplace behind:

- Had a great idea or passion they wanted to pursue.

- Wanted the challenge of independently accomplishing their own professional goals.

- Got tired of drawing a salary while making someone else rich.

- Became bored with their work and hated coming to an office daily to engage in a 9-to-5 work routine.

- Wanted control over what they did and their own destinies.

- Worked for jerks; others were victims of organizational politics, downsizings, rightsizings, layoffs, mergers, acquisitions, reorganizations, etc.

- Experienced difficulty working in an environment structured by employers whom they considered less than competent.

- Couldn't work for others; rather, they had to be in charge of their work and their own professional lives.

- Fell into their entrepreneurial venture by luck or happenstance.

- Wanted to do something really interesting after retiring.

- Answered a nagging life-changing question about their purpose: *"Is there more to life than this?"*

Necessary Skills and Competencies

Succeeding as an entrepreneur requires that you develop a wealth of skills and competencies well beyond just the product or service that you're delivering to your customers. It's not enough to be a great mechanical engineer who is starting a machine shop. You must also be a bookkeeper, salesperson, customer-service representative, purchasing agent, inventory clerk, quality inspector, administrator, and much more.

Every entrepreneur—at least at the start of any entrepreneurial venture—must wear many hats and be responsible for a numerous business functions. The good news is, as your business grows and prospers, you'll be able to hire individuals to assume many of these responsibilities which will allow you to focus on what it is that you do best (e.g., engineering, management, sales, finance, IT).

Entrepreneurial Success Circle

This pie chart provides a quick overview of how you can expect to divide your time and manage all of your entrepreneurial roles and responsibilities. Note that "Primary Line of Business" refers to what your business does, offers, produces, or delivers.

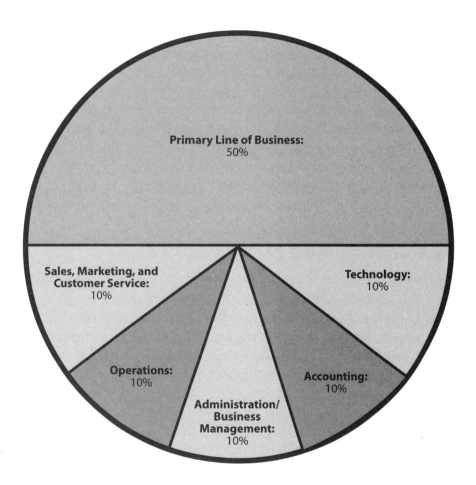

This book provides the groundwork for what you need to know in order to succeed as an entrepreneur. We'll explore all the key operating and management functions essential to the profitable growth of your business, and I'll provide you with the systems, structure, and practical information you must know to pave your way to a $100,000+ career.

I recommend that you read this book in chapter sequence in order to master all of the key elements for entrepreneurial success. And, hopefully, I've made it easy for you. Each of the remaining eight chapters focuses on one of the core entrepreneurial functions and competencies:

- Chapter 2   Positioning Yourself
- Chapter 3   Business Planning
- Chapter 4   Sales, Marketing, and Business Development
- Chapter 5   Customer Relationship Management
- Chapter 6   Money and Finance
- Chapter 7   Technology
- Chapter 8   Business Operations
- Chapter 9   Time Management and Productivity
- Chapter 10   Long-Term Entrepreneurial Success

Your challenge is to begin to master all of the concepts and strategies presented in this book, write your business plan, develop your sales and marketing programs, implement best-in-class customer-service practices, develop your budgets, project your costs, build your financial infrastructure, acquire and learn your technology, establish your operating procedures, and much more. If you follow the advice presented in this book, you will be able to build and launch your new business in just 90 days. Then you can devote the next five, 10, or 20 years to building your business, making money, and reaping the many rewards of your own entrepreneurial career.

2 Position Yourself for Entrepreneurial Success

T HERE ARE TWO IMPORTANT activities you must engage in before you decide to launch your own business. These activities will be critical to your success—building your start-up venture and managing the growth of your business.

First, you must thoroughly explore your goals and motivations. Ask yourself these important questions:

- What do I want to do?

- What do I do well?

- What do I enjoy doing?

- What makes me happy?

- What satisfies me professionally?

Research studies have shown that the most successful entrepreneurial ventures are those that are closely linked to the owner's interests, goals, motivators, and competencies. For example, it's much easier to launch a retail toy store if you're been in the retail industry in the past and know how the business works. It's much more difficult to leverage that same background into a high-tech business offering networking solutions to corporate clients. In a situation like this, the learning curve can be phenomenal and a huge obstacle to your success.

The second, and equally important, activity is to research different types of businesses in order to better understand the advantages and disadvantages of each, processes and procedures specific to each particular business or industry, potential obstacles, competitive factors, market indicators, and much more. Talk to business owners about their work, their successes, their failures, and their forecasts, and try to learn as much as possible about the reality of owning *that* type of business before you ever invest your time and money. This advice can be extremely valuable in helping you determine which businesses to avoid and which businesses might be the best fit for you, your skills, experiences, and motivators.

You should evaluate business opportunities in much the same way that you would evaluate a potential job offer. Do your research, develop your network of contacts, and conduct informational interviews to learn about your business or industry of choice. You'll be surprised and delighted to learn that most business people, even your potential competitors, will be happy to share their experiences with you and provide advice, referrals, and

You should evaluate business opportunities in the same way you'd evaluate a job offer.

other essential information. (Remember, people always love to talk about themselves and their successes!) These interactions will help you to avoid the same mistakes that hundreds, if not thousands, of others have made when starting their own businesses.

More often than not, people simply get an idea, leap into business thinking they will be great, and then learn it was neither right for them nor did they have realistic expectations about all that was involved. This is precisely why so many businesses fail each year. Don't be high on motivation but low on knowledge and skills, for thinking big is no substitute for doing the hard work. Starting and managing a business—and the myriad of functions and details—is hard work!

Learning to Manage the Risk

Every successful entrepreneur knows that starting a new business means taking risks—financial risks, personal risks, and professional risks. Therefore, you must ask yourself if you can comfortably live with these risks before you ever consider launching your own business venture. Ask yourself these questions:

- Can I live with an unstable income for the first year, two, or more of my business?

- Do I have enough money saved to sustain my personal life and my family while my business becomes established and starts to generate profits?

- Can I manage the stress and volatility associated with entrepreneurship?

- Will my family be supportive, even if things are difficult financially?

- Will my family understand that I will have very long workdays and an erratic work schedule?

- Am I willing to stake my professional reputation and career on my new venture?

If you can answer yes to all of these questions, then you're poised to launch your own business and should be able to comfortably manage the risks involved. If, on the other hand, your answer is no to several of these questions, then take some time to evaluate whether or not entrepreneurship is truly your best career choice. The risk will always exist and there is no way around the risk, no matter how spectacular your business idea.

The American Entrepreneur

Consider for a moment the implications of these business statistics:

- There are approximately 25 million small businesses in the U.S.
- The U.S. boasts the highest rate of entrepreneurship in the industrialized world.
- Small-business owners disproportionately earn more than $100,000 a year.
- Nearly 700,000 new businesses are started each year.
- 7% of Americans launch their own businesses.

- 4.5 million businesses are owned by veterans (18% of all businesses in the U.S.)
- Nearly one in 14 workers attempts to start a business each year.

There is also a downside to those business growth numbers:

- 540,000 businesses close each year.
- 50% of new businesses fail within the first three years.

You can interpret these aggregate statistics in different ways. First, you're joining a large group of like-minded individuals who want to start their own businesses. Second, such ventures have a high probability of failure. Consequently, you might conclude that starting a business is very risky because of the high failure rate. However, failure rates may not be as high as they appear in government reports. The truth is that in America it is very easy to both open and close a business.

Indeed, you could easily start two or three businesses tomorrow—most likely sole proprietorships—with minimal start-up costs. Your business may not take much capital nor demand much of your time. After letting one of your businesses languish unattended, you may decide to close it. When this business "fails" in this manner, what might that say about those 500,000+ other recorded business failures each year? In many cases, they may not be all that significant to their owners. Indeed, they disappear with less than a whimper.

My point is very simple. Don't let the general business start-up failure statistics affect your decision to start a business. What's most important are your attitudes, motivators, and skills for entrepreneurial success—success factors we'll examine in subsequent chapters.

Look for New Opportunities

Analysts, government officials, and others expect the decade ahead to be another strong period for entrepreneurship in America and throughout the world. Millions of small businesses will develop in response to new opportunities in the high-tech and service industries, the two fastest-growing industries in the U.S. (according to the Bureau of Labor Statistics).

In addition, given major issues such as energy, the environment, health care, fitness, and leisure, and the changing demographic structure, numerous opportunities are arising for small personal-service businesses to meet the needs of the elderly and career-oriented families. Businesses relating to restaurants, home maintenance, health care, housing, green technologies, energy, the environment, and mortuaries and cemeteries should continue to expand considerably over the next decade and longer.

Opportunities are also available for inventive business people who can make more productive use of busy people's time—for example, fast food, financial planning, and mail-order Internet and catalog shopping. The information and high-tech revolutions are taking place at the same time that most two-career families do not have time to waste standing in lines at banks, grocery stores, and department stores. Mail-order and Internet-based home and office-based shopping should increase dramatically during the next decade.

Identify a business that is a good fit for you, rather than one you might fit into.

Knowing the trends and opportunities is important, but they should not be the only determining factors in choosing a business. As mentioned earlier, start by identifying a business that is a good fit for you, rather than one you might fit into. Finding the right entrepreneurial venture is critical to your long-term success, financial stability, and happiness.

True to American tradition, self-employment and start-up businesses will remain great frontiers in the decades ahead.

Do You Have the "Right Stuff" to be a Successful Entrepreneur?

Do you have what it takes to become a successful and profitable entrepreneur? As you may suspect, no one has a magical success formula for the aspiring entrepreneur—only advice based on their own experiences, the experiences of others, and relevant research and statistical data. We do know why many businesses fail and we can identify some basic characteristics for success.

One of the very best places to start evaluating your potential as an entrepreneur is the Small Business Administration's website, especially the useful section on determining whether or not you are well suited for the entrepreneurial life:

http://www.sba.gov/smallbusinessplanner/plan/getready/
serv_sbplanner_isentforu.html

Characteristics of the Successful Entrepreneur

Research studies continue to identify **personal drive**—the need to achieve or the fear of failure—as a key characteristic of successful entrepreneurs. Passionate, purpose-driven people have a very high energy level and are hard-working individuals who are willing to commit themselves 100% to their business ventures. They are not daunted by challenges or obstacles; rather, they are motivated to meet those challenges and overcome those obstacles.

Other common characteristics of the successful entrepreneur include the following:

- **Able to multi-task.** Being an entrepreneur means managing a diversity of business functions on a near-daily basis. This will include business planning, marketing, sales, customer-relationship management, finance, budgeting, cost control, technology, staffing, and much more. For a graphic representation of all that it takes to succeed as an entrepreneur, refer to page 5.

- **Believe in themselves and their capabilities.** Many 80/20 individuals succeed as entrepreneurs. Basically, this tenet states that 80% of positive changes and movement in the business world result from the most powerful 20% of actions, ideas, and innovators (entrepreneurs). In essence, these 20% discovered what they do better than anyone else and they worked it to their maximum advantage. You can think of Oprah, Bill Gates, Jeff Bezos, and others as examples of powerful 80/20 individuals.

- **Share a common mindset.** Simply put, they view themselves as entrepreneurs and not as their job (e.g., mechanic, engineer, writer, graphic designer, funeral director, coach). They believe that they are successful entrepreneurs, for they must believe it before anyone else will.

- **Take risks.** You will find few challenges riskier and more time-consuming than starting your own company. It involves a lot of hard work, long hours, and a significant financial risk—betting on your financial future. At the same time, you may experience your greatest professional satisfaction in running your own business, especially if you are pursuing your passion.

- **Have realistic expectations.** They do not expect to make a million dollars the first year; they do not expect their businesses to be standard, efficient, and profitable every single day.

- **See security in themselves.** They understand that their employment security lies within themselves and what they can do and accomplish.

- **Act with confidence and self-reliance.** Although most successful entrepreneurs surround themselves with the experts they need (e.g., accountant, financial planner, attorney, business advisor, staff), they are confident in their abilities and rely on their gut instinct to make sound business decisions based on factual information.

- **Adapt to change by being flexible.** Starting a new venture means constant change and adaptation. If you're rigid and unyielding, you'll find that an entrepreneurial career may not be the right choice for you. Successful business owners know that they need to constantly respond to changes in market conditions, economic indicators, competitive forces, client expectations, and more.

- **Handle uncertainty with ease.** Successful entrepreneurs know that unpredictability is the status quo. Markets change, economies change, product requirements change, service requirements change…the list goes on and on. And, unfortunately, many of these changes are not predictable. As such, small-business owners need to constantly educate themselves about their businesses, products, services, and industries, and pay close attention to changes in trends and business cycles in order to maximize their performance.

- **Become dedicated, driven, and disciplined.** They are willing to forego the family outing on Saturday to work on a deadline-driven project; they are willing to drag themselves out of bed at 4 am to complete a client project due for delivery that day; and, they are willing to spend hour after hour analyzing financial statements when they'd rather be out golfing.

- **Willing to make sacrifices to ensure the success of their venture**. This might mean not buying that new car for another year or two, missing out on a great vacation in order to be sure they have enough money to cover payroll for the next month, or asking their children to attend a state university instead of a $40,000+ per year private college. Remember, entrepreneurship can require sacrifices from you and from your family members.

- **Look within themselves for strengths.** Entrepreneurs often find their greatest strength and power within themselves. They are often not team players, but rather independent, capable, goal-directed individuals who know what motivates them, are able to harness that energy, and are able to move forward despite any apparent obstacles. They are confident within themselves and confident about their capabilities.

Evaluate Your Entrepreneurial Drive and Skills

On pages 15-19 you'll find two checklists that are essential to helping you determine whether or not you have the personal and professional skills, competencies, attitudes, and talents that are critical for your success as an entrepreneur. The first checklist—"Entrepreneurial Spirit and Drive"—focuses on the personal characteristics that are essential to your entrepreneurial success. The second checklist—"Entrepreneurial Toolkit of Skills and Competencies"—will help you evaluate which skills you currently possess and which skills you will need to develop to ensure your successful performance.

Be sure to take the time that is necessary to honestly complete both of these checklists, for they will provide you with a foundation on which to build your skills and competencies to ensure your long-term entrepreneurial success.

Defining Your Business

Your decision on how to get started in business and what type of business to launch should be based largely on your specific skills, talents, and objectives. Once you're clear and focused about what you have to bring to the table, then you can better evaluate the various options available to launch your entrepreneurial career.

1. **Start your own business from scratch.** This option is probably what most people think of when you talk about entrepreneurial ventures. It's you, your idea, and your hard work. However, do consider the fact that many new businesses are launched

Entrepreneurial Drive and Spirit

	YES	NO
1. Do you have drive?	❑	❑
2. Are you self-disciplined?	❑	❑
3. Are you determined to succeed?	❑	❑
4. Do you have a positive attitude?	❑	❑
5. Are you focused and diligent?	❑	❑
6. Are you charismatic and enthusiastic?	❑	❑
7. Are you creative and imaginative?	❑	❑
8. Do you consider yourself a visionary?	❑	❑
9. Do you have a tremendous amount of energy?	❑	❑
10. Are you smart?	❑	❑
11. Do you have top-flight morals, ethics, and integrity?	❑	❑
12. Are you willing to work harder than you ever have before?	❑	❑
13. Are you patient?	❑	❑
14. Are you flexible?	❑	❑
15. Is your family supportive?	❑	❑
16. Can you take constructive criticism without becoming offended?	❑	❑
17. Can you think independently?	❑	❑
18. Can you make decisions?	❑	❑
19. Can you solve problems?	❑	❑
20. Do you thrive in challenging and fast-paced environments?	❑	❑
21. Can you handle the constant change and realignment that any new venture requires?	❑	❑
22. Are you able to work without supervision?	❑	❑
23. Can you handle disappointment and then move on?	❑	❑
24. Are you willing to learn from your mistakes?	❑	❑
25. Do you believe that you can always learn from others?	❑	❑

	YES	NO
26. Are you well-organized and efficient?	☐	☐
27. Are you consistently productive?	☐	☐
28. Are you committed to uncompromising quality?	☐	☐
29. Do you have good written communication skills?	☐	☐
30. Do you have strong oral communication skills?	☐	☐
31. Are you comfortable speaking in public?	☐	☐
32. Are you "hungry" to succeed?	☐	☐
33. Do you have the financial resources to support yourself during the start-up phases of your new venture?	☐	☐
34. Can you persevere through difficult times?	☐	☐
35. Can you handle adversity?	☐	☐
36. Can you live comfortably in a high-risk employment situation?	☐	☐
37. Are you willing to make the necessary sacrifices?	☐	☐
38. Do you understand that calculated risks can lead to tremendous rewards?	☐	☐
39. Can your mind and your body handle unusually large amounts of stress?	☐	☐
40. Does a great deal of your self-image come from your work?	☐	☐
41. Do you crave success and self-satisfaction?	☐	☐
42. Are you ready NOW?	☐	☐

If you answered "Yes" to more than 25 of the 42 questions, you do have the entrepreneurial drive and spirit that is critical to building any successful new business or consulting practice. I congratulate you and urge you to move forward. You're hungry, you're committed, and you're ready! Go for it!

If you answered "Yes" to fewer than 25 qustions, you need to seriously reexamine your interest in becoming an entrepreneur. Your answers to this questionnaire indicate that you may not be ready to make the transition from "employee" to "entrepreneur."

Entrepreneurial Skills and Competencies

		YES	NO
1.	I have clearly defined my expertise and business concept.	☐	☐
2.	My business fills a specific market need.	☐	☐
3.	I believe in my heart that my proposed business venture will be successful.	☐	☐
4.	I have determined which business model is most ppropriate for my line of work—a "C" corporation, an "S" corporation, a sole proprietorship, a partnership, a joint venture, or another business entity.	☐	☐
5.	I have sought legal counsel to help me set up my business and manage it according to federal, state, and local regulations.	☐	☐
6.	I have written a formal business plan.	☐	☐
7.	I have shared my business concept with others to get their feedback.	☐	☐
8.	I have identified a specific market for my services and/or products.	☐	☐
9.	I have identified my targeted customer markets.	☐	☐
10.	I know who my competition is, what they do, and what they charge.	☐	☐
11.	I have selected a location for my business.	☐	☐
12.	I have an advertising and marketing plan in place.	☐	☐
13.	I have written and designed my marketing communications (e.g., sales brochures, product literature, advertisements, promotions).	☐	☐
14.	I have developed a website.	☐	☐
15.	I have set up a business email account so that customers can easily contact me.	☐	☐
16.	I have set up a business phone line and sourced the most cost-effective providers for both local and long-distance services.	☐	☐

	YES	NO
17. I have prepared budget, revenue, and income projections.	❑	❑
18. I have set up systems that will ensure stringent control over all expenses so that I know precisely where my money is being spent.	❑	❑
19. I have set up systems to track revenues, what markets or types of customers they're coming from, and which revenue streams are most profitable.	❑	❑
20. I have sought the advice of an accountant, tax specialist, or financial consultant to help me set up my business and put all the right systems in place.	❑	❑
21. I have set up a business bank account and/or a money-market account.	❑	❑
22. I have evaluated the savings and investment options available for entrepreneurs.	❑	❑
23. I have set up the business as a merchant to accept credit-card payments.	❑	❑
24. I have written the operating policies and procedures to effectively manage and control my business.	❑	❑
25. I know what technology I will require to establish and deliver my products and/or services.	❑	❑
26. I know what equipment, materials, and other resources that I need to purchase to launch my new venture.	❑	❑
27. I know what equipment, technology, materials, and resources I will need to acquire in order to manage and build my business over time.	❑	❑
28. I have good networking and relationship-development skills that are essential to building cooperative alliances with customers, vendors, creditors, and bankers.	❑	❑
29. I have designed a preliminary work schedule for myself that is comfortable for both me and my family.	❑	❑
30. I have thought about where I'd like my business to be in five years, 10 years, and longer.	❑	❑

	YES	NO
31. I have clearly defined my business goals and expectations for long-term growth, expansion, and/or diversification.	❏	❏
32. I have considered my long-term business exit strategy so that, at some point, I'll have earned enough money to be able to retire or sell my business.	❏	❏

It is not our expectation, nor should it be yours, that you will have already developed all of the 32 skills and competencies required for the start-up of a successful entrepreneurial venture. Rather, this checklist is designed to alert you to the specific areas in which you need to focus your energies and develop your talents to ensure the professional and financial success of your business.

as a partnership between two or more individuals, leveraging the strengths, knowledge, connections, and capabilities of all parties to spur business development, growth, and success.

2. **Buy an established business.** There are tens of thousands, if not more, businesses for sale every day. Just look in the newspaper or on the Internet, or talk to a business broker. Opportunities abound. It's a great way to get your business up and running quickly, but will often require a substantial capital investment. Be sure you have the money on hand or are comfortable borrowing the money and know that you can repay the debt.

3. **Join a direct-sales company.** There are hundreds, if not thousands, of direct-sales companies including some very well-known ones such as Avon, Mary Kay, Shaklee, and Creative Memories. This industry has matured over the past several decades and is now enjoying tremendous success and favor within the market. If this is the type of entrepreneurial venture you might be interested in, carefully research all of your options to find the best fit for you.

4. **Purchase a franchise.** Buying a franchise is like buying a "business in a box" with complete instructions for set-up and operation. In many regards, it couldn't be easier. The major drawback to this type of venture is the initial capital investment and the ongoing financial obligation throughout the entire life of the franchise. If you're considering this type of venture, I recommend intensive research to identify the right opportunity and expert legal counsel as you negotiate the contracts.

5. **Accept employment with an existing business that's offering you an equity/ownership opportunity.** If entrepreneurship appeals to you, yet you're hesitant to make that big leap, you might consider joining a company that will offer you an equity (or ownership) interest as part of your compensation package. A rare occurrence in years past, this is now becoming a much more common practice as companies realize that individuals with a vested financial interest in the performance of the company will work harder, longer, and more diligently so that everyone succeeds.

6. **Succeed into a family-owned business.** For those of you who were fortunate enough to have been born into a family that already owns and operates a business, *you* may very well be that company's succession plan . . . the next individual to take the helm. As with all family relationships, this can have its plusses and its minuses, and only you can determine if this is the right entrepreneurial career option for you.

You'll read much more about these various types of entrepreneurial ventures in the next chapter.

Defining Your Business Model

Another key consideration in determining which type of business is most appropriate for you and your skill sets is the type of business model you'll be most comfortable operating. This may vary widely from one individual to another, so it's important that you consider the unique characteristics of each model and the foundation on which it is built to determine which is right for you.

Most businesses operate according to one of three different models:

1. **Customer-Centric.** These types of businesses focus primarily on delivering products and/or services to their customers. Examples include professional-service businesses, technology-consulting firms, in-home health care, and janitorial and cleaning services.

2. **Economic-Centric.** These types of businesses focus primarily on volume—of products, of services, and of money. Examples include retail stores, online stores, and financial sales.

3. **Service-Centric.** These types of business are customer-focused with an economic/diversification twist. Examples include resume-writing firms that also offer career coaching, interviewing training, and other job-search services in partnership with other companies. It's a great model to expand your product and service offerings by leverging the talents of others.

It is important to note that every business is really based on a combination of all three of the above-referenced business models. The true distinction lies in which of the three is the dominant model in your particular venture.

We'll further examine these various types of businesses and business models in Chapter 3.

Research Is Your Most Powerful Tool

Once you have decided which type of entrepreneurial venture is appropriate for you, it's now time to do extensive research so that you can learn as much as possible about the business and industry you'll be entering. Years ago, this would have required weeks, if not months, of research in the library as you attempted to collect as much information as possible. Today, however, the Internet has made research easy and gives you the ability to capture vast amounts of information extraordinarily fast and become remarkably better educated about "everything"—from different industries, markets, products, services, and solutions to information about every core business function (e.g., sales, marketing, human resources, strategic planning, vendor sourcing, import/export, manufacturing, distribution, transportation, technology tools, sales negotiations).

Just as important, you'll want to network with as many people as possible in the business that you're considering. As we discussed earlier in this chapter, you'll be amazed at how many people will be willing to share their business and industry expertise with you. All you need to do is ask!

Building Your Entrepreneurial Success Team

No one, not even an entrepreneur, operates in total isolation. In fact, everyone needs a community that will support them, advise them, guide them, inspire them, and challenge them. Successful entrepreneurs already know that and have most likely already established their entrepreneurial success team.

As you begin the initial planning phases of your new business, you'll need to immediately begin assembling a team who can provide you with the expertise and knowledge that you'll need to succeed. For some, these individuals may form the core of your Board of Directors. For others, these individuals will be your lifeline, your support system, and your professional community.

You should consider including the following types of individuals and organizations on your team:

- **Accountant/CPA/Financial Advisor.** Unless you're an accountant or financial expert by trade, I cannot stress enough the importance of getting sound financial advice. This alone can make the difference between entrepreneurial success and entrepreneurial defeat.

- **Attorney.** The legalities and regulations of owning and operating your own business become more and more complex with each passing year. As such, sound legal advice is a must for every entrepreneur, even if only to help you set up your company according to federal, state, and local regulations, and then be sure that you submit all required documentation each year.

- **Professional Mentor/Business Coach.** Having your own mentor or coach is like having a cheerleader on your side, every step of the way. This, in and of itself, gives you an instant advantage when launching a new venture and continuing to manage its operations as it grows, develops, and expands. When you have an expert advisor, you have an individual who can help you make difficult decisions, evaluate your options and opportunities, be brutally honest with you, and introduce you to others who may be important to your success.

- **Professional Colleagues.** Your network of professional colleagues can be a tremendous source of knowledge, support, and inspiration. Leverage them to your advantage and, remember, they'll most likely be honored that you asked for their assistance and contribution. Build colleagues, not competitors.

- **Professional Associations.** Membership in relevant professional associations will allow you to amass a wealth of information about particular industries, professions, customer markets, and more, not to mention the great professional contacts you'll develop.

- **Friends and Family.** Your personal network of friends, neighbors, and family members will always be a source of inspiration and support through the entire lifecycle of your business, from the initial excitement of planning and start-up, through the long and lonely hours of frustration, to the joys of financial and professional success. Be certain that these individuals are valued contributors to your entrepreneurial success team.

Avoid Common Entrepreneurial Pitfalls

The top three reasons that new businesses fail are poor planning, poor management, and poor decision making. Other common reasons include:

- Insufficient market research
- Undercapitalization
- Poor location
- Inflexibility
- Extremely high and debilitating costs
- Poor understanding of accounting, finance, and economics
- Lack of owner commitment
- Disorganization and inability to follow up
- Unwillingness to sacrifice
- Inability to make difficult decisions

- Unwillingness to make business changes despite poor performance
- Lack of interpersonal relationship and communication skills
- Lack of necessary sales and business-development skills
- Lack of leadership skills
- Inability to solve problems
- Poor performance in employee hiring, training, and motivation
- Not charging what products or services are worth
- Not seeking appropriate legal and financial guidance
- Bad luck or poor timing

Another major reason for failure is that individuals launch new ventures for negative, rather than positive, reasons. Perhaps they were fired, hated their jobs, couldn't find work, or needed immediate income. If you find yourself in this situation, be careful about making a decision to launch your own business. That type of life-altering decision is best made from a position of power and positive thinking, and not because you're feeling desperate.

This book will address all of these issues and more, providing you with practical, actionable information and resources that you can use to ensure that you don't fall victim to these common reasons for business failure.

Great Entrepreneurial Resources

The following books represent some of the best resources for the start-up entrepreneur:

- *101 Small Business Ideas for Under $5,000* (Corey Sandler and Janice Keefe)
- *199 Great Home Businesses You Can Start (and Succeed In) for Under $1,000* (Tyler Hicks)
- *Adams Streetwise Small Business Start-Up* (Bob Adams)
- *Barron's Dictionary of Business Terms* (Jack P. Friedman)

- *The Book of Entrepreneurs' Wisdom: Classic Writings by Legendary Entrepreneurs* (Peter Krass, Editor)
- *Buffettology* (Mary Buffet and David Clark)
- *Business Plans Kit For Dummies* (Steven D. Peterson and Peter E. Jaret)
- *Finding Your Perfect Work* (Paul and Sarah Edwards)
- *Franchising For Dummies* (Michael Seid)
- *The Great Game of Business* (Jack Stack)
- *Have You Got What It Takes? The Entrepreneur's Complete Self-Assessment Guide* (Doug Gray)
- *How to Buy, Sell, and Profit on eBay* (Adam Ginsberg)
- *How to Start, Run, and Stay in Business* (Gregory F. Kishel and Patricia Gunter Kishel)
- *Home-Based Business for Dummies* (Paul Edwards, Sarah Edwards and Peter Economy)
- *Kick Start Your Dream Business: Getting It Started and Keeping You Going* (Romanus Wolter)
- *Made in America* (Sam Walton)
- *Six-Week Start-Up* (Rhonda Abrams)
- *Small Business Kit for Dummies* (Richard D. Harroch)
- *Small Business Marketing for Dummies* (Barbara Findlay Schenck)
- *The Small Business Start-Up Kit* (Peri Pakroo and Barbara Kate Repa)
- *Small-Time Operator* (Bernard B. Kamoroff)
- *The Successful Business Plan* (Rhonda Abrams and Eugene Kleiner)
- *The Warren Buffet Way* (Robert G. Hagstrom, Jr.)
- *The Way to the Top* (Donald Trump)
- *What Business Should I Start?* (Rhonda Abrams and Scott Cook)
- *What No One Ever Tells You About Starting Your Own Business* (Jan Norman)

- *You Need to Be a Little Crazy: The Truth About Starting and Growing Your Business* (Barry Moltz)

There are also thousands of online resources with a wealth of information about starting and running your own business. Several of my favorites include:

■ **AllBusiness**	*www.allbusiness.com*
■ **BizMove.com**	*http://bizmove.com*
■ **Business Know-How**	*http://businessknowhow.com*
■ **My Own Business**	*www.myownbusiness.org*
■ **Small Business Administration**	*www.sba.gov/smallbusinessplanner/ start/index.html*
■ **Startup Journal**	*www.startupjournal.com*

The federal government will help you with several publications available through the Small Business Administration (SBA). Check out the "Library" section on the SBA website where you'll find 200+ free publications, including e-books that you can immediately download, as well as numerous resource links related to launching a new business.

www.sba.gov/tools/resourcelibrary/index.html

The Internal Revenue Service (*www.irs.gov*) offers a great deal of tax and accounting information for start-up businesses. The U.S. Chamber of Commerce (*www.uschamber.com*), as well as its local chapters, also offer useful information.

Other valuable online resources to help you start a business include:

■ **American Express Open**	*https://home.americanexpress. com/home/open.shtml*
■ **Business Owner's Toolkit**	*http://toolkit.cch.com*
■ **CEO Business Express**	*www.ceoexpress.com/default.asp*
■ **Entrepreneur.com**	*www.entrepreneur.com*
■ **Kaufmann eVenturing**	*www.eventuring.org*
■ **EWeb**	*http://eweb.slu.edu*
■ **Home Biz Tools**	*http://homebiztools.com*

- Inc.com   *www.inc.com/guides/start_biz*
- SCORE   *www.score.org*
- Yahoo Small Business   *http://smallbusiness.yahoo.com*

For Veterans Only

Numerous government agencies and nonprofit organizations offer a wealth of specialized assistance to veterans interested in starting their own businesses. Most of the assistance involves training, counseling, and financing. If you're a veteran, be sure to explore the following websites and programs designed specifically for you:

- **Center for Veterans Enterprise**   *www.vetbiz.gov*
- **HireVetsFirst**   *www.hirevetsfirst.gov/ smallbizown.asp*
- **Office of Veterans Business Development (SBA)**   *www.sba.gov/aboutsba/ sbaprograms/ovbd/ index.html*
- **The Veterans Corporation**   *www.veteranscorp.com*
- **Veterans' Business Outreach Center (VBOC)**   *www.vboc.org*
- **Veterans Business Network**   *www.veteransbusiness network.com*
- **VetFriends**   *www.vetfriends.com*

3 Even Columbus Needed a Map

EVERY BUSINESS OWNER NEEDS a business plan. In fact, if you're reading this book while in the start-up stages of launching your own enterprise, your business plan should be one of the very first things that you do. Although it may seem a daunting task, a business plan will continue to be a valuable guide as you develop, build, and expand your business.

You may think that all of your handwritten notes, index cards, Post-It notes, and piles of paper are enough to get your business off the ground and moving forward. Trust me, however, when I tell that you it's simply not enough. A formal business plan is your roadmap to success. Without it, how will you know which direction to go?

This chapter will provide you with the resources and information you need in order to develop a solid business plan. However, prior to writing your business plan there are several critical decisions that you must make:

- **What type of business do you plan to start?** Will it be retail, manufacturing, transportation, professional services, health care, the arts, consumer products, or automotive? The list goes on and on.

- **What are your various options for launching your new venture?** Should you start a business from scratch, acquire an existing business, purchase a franchise, or consider other opportunities?

- **What type of business model are you going to use?** Will your business focus on the one-on-one customer relationship or on the volume of products and/or services that you can sell?

I'll explore each of these three issues in detail, and then move on to the intricacies of writing your business plan.

Selecting Your Business Type

The very first step in launching your own business is to determine what type of business you want. At first, you may think that this will be an easy decision, but once you begin researching your options, you'll find that the list of possibilities is virtually endless. As such, you must commit yourself to a thorough investigation to explore all realistic opportunities before you actually begin to invest your time, money, and expertise into starting your own entrepreneurial venture.

Most people determine which type of business to start based on one of three different criteria:

- **Professional skills and competencies.** For example, an individual with a wealth of experience in logistics may start a warehousing and distribution business.

- **Personal passions.** Consider the beverage sales manager who, after 20+ years in the field, has now decided to start a fine-arts gallery based on his lifelong experience as a painter and his interest in the arts. How wonderful to turn something you really enjoy—a hobby or avocation—into a profitable, fun, and rewarding new venture.

- **Projected performance of the market, the economy, and/or a particular industry.** Consider the purchasing agent who determines that an Internet-based bookstore offering e-publications will be a sure winner in the decade ahead and moves forward with that venture.

The best of all worlds would be an entrepreneurial venture that meets all three of the above criteria—a business that utilizes your core skills and competencies which ties directly to your passion, and is in an industry or field which is projected to have strong growth throughout the coming years. Here's a great example:

> When Sarah graduated from college years ago, she knew that she wanted a career in the social-services industry where she would have the opportunity to make a positive impact on the lives of others. Following graduation, she began her career as a geriatric social worker where, for the past 10 years, she's been rapidly promoted through a series of increasingly responsible positions.
>
> Although Sarah's commitment and passion have not changed over the years and, in fact, she's more motivated than ever to make a difference in the quality of life of our aging population, she's ready to leave the drudgery of the 9-5 workforce to pursue her own venture as a private consultant to social-service agencies nationwide. This would be an ideal scenario, combining Sarah's core skills and motivating passions into a business that is poised for strong and sustainable growth (as predicted by the U.S. Bureau of Labor Statistics).

Service businesses in general, such as the geriatric social-service consulting firm just mentioned, offer some of the strongest entrepreneurial opportunities in the global economy. Service businesses are particularly attractive because they're the fastest to establish, normally require only a small initial investment, and are relatively easy to manage from both operational and financial perspectives. In fact, many of these types of ventures can be operated from your home, which keeps your overhead and operating costs to a minimum.

Research all your options before you invest your time, money, and expertise.

High-tech businesses are also predicted to be strong performers over the next decade. Although we've recently experienced the dot-com bust and its negative impact on our economy and on many small businesses, statistics from sources worldwide indicate that there will be strong growth within diverse high-tech sectors for many years to come. If high-tech products, services, and/or solutions are your expertise, this type of business venture may be ideal for you.

On the opposite side of the continuum, **manufacturing businesses** in the U.S. (outside of the high-tech arena) are projected to have the slowest level of growth over the next decade. More and more companies are offshoring their production operations to other countries where labor costs are phenomenally less expensive than in the U.S. The entire industry is changing, shifting, and moving in new directions. This, in and of itself, adds a new risk for start-up businesses in the manufacturing sector. What's more, manufacturing businesses usually require a significant capital investment for facilities, equipment, materials, employees, and more. Be certain that you have the financial resources, product expertise, industry connections, leadership capabilities, and more before you enter this highly competitive and cost-driven marketplace.

Selecting Your Best Entrepreneurial Option

Once you've made the decision as to what type of business you want to launch, and you're clear about why a particular business or industry is the right one for you, then it's time to move on to the second phase of your business-planning efforts. This phase—selecting the best entrepreneurial option—is vitally important and will lay the foundation for everything else you do as you begin to move forward with your new venture.

Each of these six options has distinct advantages and disadvantages as you'll read about:

1. **Start your own business from scratch.** This option is probably what most people think of when you talk about entrepreneurial ventures. It's you, your idea, and your hard work. You have total control of your business, work life, and destiny. If you can build a successful venture, you'll hopefully enjoy the many financial and professional rewards. But you'll also have total responsibility for everything that happens in your business—the good and the bad. It's the typical high-risk, high-reward scenario that most people think of as entrepreneurship.

   More and more start-up entrepreneurs are considering the advantages of business partnerships that provide for shared responsibilities between two or more owners. These types of businesses can overcome the many obstacles and potential isolation of a single-owner entrepreneurial venture, and leverage the strengths, knowledge, connections, and capabilities of all parties to spur business development, growth, and success.

   Taking it one step further, you might also consider other unique, partnership-type relationships such as strategic alliances, joint

ventures, co-marketing agreements, and more. These cooperative relationships allow multiple companies to work together to everyone's
mutual advantage.

2. **Buy an established business.** If you go to *google.com* and search
   for "businesses for sale," you'll get 106 million results, ranging
   from a ranching company in Boise to a parking-garage operation
   in Baltimore to a high-tech design firm in San Francisco. Obviously, you'll want to narrow your search significantly, but the results
   clearly demonstrate what a huge market exists for the purchase of
   an established company. Next, add into that mix a search through
   your local newspaper and you'll identify even more opportunities. Then, contact business brokers to see what companies they
   may currently have for sale. The list of places to look and people
   to talk to is endless as the supply of available businesses is endless.

   The true advantage to acquiring an existing company is obvious
   —the business is already up and running, employees are in place,
   customers already exist, products and/or services are being delivered,
   and the financial performance of the company is well documented.
   When you take this avenue to entrepreneurship, you bypass much
   of the start-up phase that all new business owners go through
   whenever they launch a new venture, and that can be great news.

   Conversely, acquiring a business requires a capital investment.
   Simply put, you have to pay! This may only be a few thousand dollars
   if you're buying a small business, or can be a huge amount of money
   if you're purchasing a large corporation. In this situation, either you
   have to have saved enough money to fund the investment yourself
   or be able to borrow the money from a bank, family member, or
   private investor. If you do borrow the money, you'll put yourself into
   an immediate debt position from which you'll have to work your way
   out. As such, be certain that you have qualified legal and financial
   advice as you consider such a significant investment and liability.

   Although acquiring a business can truly be the best alternative
   for some aspiring entrepreneurs, it is also important that you have
   realistic expectations. No matter how financially and operationally
   stable a company may be, a change in ownership always has a ripple
   effect throughout the entire organization. You must be prepared to
   effectively manage that transition, accelerate the positive changes,
   and eliminate any negative impact (and, yes, there always will be
   negative impact associated with any change in ownership!).

3. **Join a direct-sales company.** Do you remember when Amway first hit the market? It was more than 45 years ago and most Americans were horrified by the concept of multi-level marketing. No one had ever tried to build this type of company on the magnitude that Amway attempted (and succeeded). Now, after several decades of instability, multi-level marketing—now referred to as direct sales—has become an established industry with a solid reputation and offers a wealth of opportunities for prospective entrepreneurs. Here's a list of just a few of the best-known direct-sales companies of today:

- **Avon**
- **Mary Kay**
- **Shaklee**
- **Creative Memories**
- **Discovery Toys**
- **Tupperware**
- **World Book**
- **Stanley Home Products**
- **Longaberger**
- **Pre-Paid Legal Services**
- **Herbalife**
- **Primerica Financial Services**
- **NuSkin**
- **The Happy Gardener**
- **Pampered Chef**
- **Home Interiors**

A quick search on the Internet for "direct-sales companies" will reveal hundreds, if not thousands, of opportunities. We recommend that you start with the following two websites, each of which lists hundreds of direct-sales companies, along with their full contact information.

- **Network Marketing Companies** — *http://www.npros.com/directory.asp*
- **Direct Selling Association** — *http://www.dsa.org*

Today, hundreds of thousands of direct-sales entrepreneurs are controlling their own destinies while making a great living. It's a combination that can't be beat! If this is the type of company you might be interested in, we recommend that you spend a great deal of time investigating all of your options to identify the company and sales structure that is just right for you. It is important to note that, just like acquiring an existing company, there will be an initial capital investment required to launch your direct-sales venture. Common fees include the purchase of the "business kit" (the know-how information, advertisements, and product literature) and an initial inventory of merchandise. The dollars involved can range dramatically, from only a few hundred dollars up to tens of thousands of dollars. Be certain that you carefully research the financial obligations and commitments that you're making when you buy into one of these firms.

4. **Purchase a franchise.** Franchises are a great way to launch your own business venture. In essence, you're buying a "business in a box" with complete instructions and support for initial set-up and long-term operation. In many regards, it couldn't be easier, assuming that you have the skills and knowledge to effectively operate and profitably manage that particular type of business. In my research, I identified thousands of companies in a wide range of industries that offer franchise opportunities. Here are just a few to demonstrate the diversity of opportunities that franchising can offer to you:

■ **McDonald's**	■ **MAACO**
■ **RE/MAX Real Estate**	■ **Hilton Hotels**
■ **Maid Brigade**	■ **Staybridge Suites**
■ **PODS**	■ **Curves**
■ **Big Picture Framing**	■ **AAMCO Transmissions**
■ **Dollar Store**	■ **Club 50 Fitness Centers**
■ **Cinnabon**	■ **Econo Lube N' Tune**
■ **Carvel**	■ **The Plant Lady**
■ **Geeks on Call**	■ **Bear Creek Coffee**
■ **eCommercials Video**	■ **Minuteman Press**
■ **GNC Live Well**	■ **Play It Again Sports**

The top 26 industries in which you will find franchising opportunities include:

■ Auto products/services	■ Jewelry
■ Business opportunities	■ Lodging
■ Business services	■ Pet-related
■ Child-related	■ Real estate
■ Cleaning	■ Retail

- Computer-related
- Entertainment
- Finance
- Food
- Golf
- Health & beauty
- Home & mobile services
- Home services
- Security
- Senior care services
- Sports
- Tanning
- Tools & equipment
- Travel
- Wholesale/distribution
- Wireless communications

The major drawback to this type of venture is the initial capital investment, which can range from under $10,000 (for a Lincoln Log Homes franchise) to approximately $1 million (for a McDonald's franchise). In addition, franchises have an ongoing financial obligation to the franchiser which can equal a large percentage of your annual revenues throughout the entire life of the franchise.

Extensive research and investigation are mandatory if you're considering this type of opportunity in order to identify a franchise that matches your skill sets, is in line with your current career goals and interests, and for which you have the requisite financial assets to acquire and operate the business. In addition, I cannot stress enough the importance of retaining an experienced franchise attorney and accountant who can provide you with critical information and insights as you move forward with your decision making and into the final stages of negotiation and franchise acquisition.

For more information on franchising, visit these websites that offer a plethora of information about franchising opportunities, investment requirements, and financial obligations:

- *www.entrepreneur.com*
- *www.franchise.com*
- *www.franchise.net*
- *www.franchise.org*
- *www.franchise50.com*
- *www.franchiseadvantage.com*
- *www.franchisedirect.com*
- *www.franchiseforsale.com*

- *www.franchisegator.com*
- *www.franchiseonline.com*
- *www.franchiseopportunities.com*
- *www.franchisesearch.com*
- *www.franchisesolutions.com*
- *http://l-h1.com/franchise_network/testpage/*
- *www.smallbusinessopportunity.com*

5. **Accept employment with an existing business that's offering you an equity/ownership opportunity.** For many aspiring entrepreneurs, accepting an equity position with an established company is a great way to begin to take the leadership reins of an organization. A rare occurrence in years past, this is now becoming a more regular practice as companies realize that individuals with a vested financial interest in the performance of the company will work harder, longer hours, and more diligently so that everyone succeeds.

   Generally, although not always, this type of entrepreneurial arrangement offers you the best of all worlds—an annual salary or compensation plan (just as a traditional employee would receive) along with an equity interest in the company. The equity interest may be a fixed ownership percentage, an ownership percentage that increases with each year, or an ownership percentage that fluctuates based on the financial performance of the company.

   This type of arrangement is considered to be a lower-risk venture than many other entrepreneurial options. Since you're joining an existing company, we expect that you've done your research to be certain that the company is on solid operational and financial ground. As such, when you accept this type of opportunity, you're guaranteed not only your salary but also ownership interest that can build over time. In fact, at some point, it may be that you (or another stakeholder) determines that you want to own the corporation independently and, therefore, may initiate a management buy-out, acquisition, or other type of action to purchase the entire company. If this is your long-term objective, there is no better way to learn the business, understand the company, and know the key players than to have worked in the business for years.

   One word of advice . . . if this is the entrepreneurial path that you wish to pursue, we strongly recommend that you enter into a business or industry in which you either have some knowledge, skills, and experience, or in which you have a personal drive and passion. Entrepreneurship, no matter the specific model, can be a tough and rocky road. The more passionate you are about what you do, the easier it will be to travel that road.

6. **Succeed into a family-owned business.** If you talk to people who were born into a business, you'll find that you get remarkably different advice. For some individuals, it's been a natural progression to move into the family business. They never considered anything else and never wanted anything else. It was a perfect fit.

   On the other side of the spectrum, however, are individuals who were forced to join a family business that they were not interested in, did not want to manage, and did not want to own. For these individuals, their professional lives have fallen short of their expectations, their desires, and their true skill sets.

   If you find yourself in this position—where you're slated to be the next individual to take over a family enterprise—we recommend that you give it intensely serious consideration. There is nothing worse that resigning yourself to 40, 50, or 60 hours a week doing something than you do not enjoy. Although it may not seem like it, everyone does have choices and you alone have the power to decide whether or not a family venture is right for you.

Defining Your Business Model

Another key consideration in determining which entrepreneurial venture is most appropriate for you and your skill sets is the type of business model you'll be most comfortable operating. This may vary widely from one individual to another, so it's important that you consider the unique characteristics of each model and the foundation on which each type of business is built in order to determine which is right for you.

The decision you make regarding your business model will significantly impact which of the preceding six types of entrepreneurial options is most in line with your style of management, your professional objectives, and your entrepreneurial goals.

There are three business models from which you can choose:

1. **Customer-Centric Model.** The foundation for these businesses is the customer (or client)—pure and simple. In fact, the entire business revolves around the customer and your ability to build and sustain

long-term, profitable client relationships. Typical businesses that fall into this category include:

- **Professional-Services Businesses** (accounting, financial consulting, legal, residential/commercial design, career coaching, psychiatric counseling)

- **Technology-Consulting Firms** (networking, website design & management, enterprise solutions, telecommunications, graphic design)

- **Personal-Service Businesses** (tailoring, child care, home cleaning, interior design)

- **General-Service Businesses** (automotive repair, HVAC, janitorial, electrical service)

If you decide to launch a customer-centric entrepreneurial venture, be certain to pay extra attention to Chapter 5, *Customers, Clients, and Patrons: Can't Live With Them; Can't Live Without Them!* This chapter provides detailed information on building, nurturing, and managing the all-important client relationship that will, ultimately, be the foundation for your success.

2. **Economic-Centric Model.** The primary driving force behind these businesses is volume—of products, of services, and of money. You want to build a venture that can deliver a significant number of products or services, while generating strong revenues and bottom-line profits. Typical businesses that fall into this category include:

- **Manufacturing Businesses** (technology, consumer products, pharmaceuticals, biomedical equipment, industrial products, refrigeration systems)

- **Retail Stores** (clothing, shoes, home goods, hardware, automotive, books, gifts, electronics)

- **Online Stores** (books, videos, CDs, clothing, linens, tools, industrial components)

- **Rental Companies** (industrial equipment, home products, landscaping equipment, automotive, computers)

For the start-up entrepreneur, the greatest challenge in building and sustaining this type of venture will be your ability to let go and relinquish control of certain operations and activities to others within your business organization. If volume is your motivating force, then most likely your business will grow, expand, and require additional staff. At some point, as the volume builds, you simply will not be able to manage it all yourself.

For many entrepreneurs, myself included, it is very difficult to let go of any responsibilities and trust that someone else will do it as well and as precisely you would. Whether that's the reality or not isn't the question. The question is whether you'll be able to hand off certain tasks to others. In fact, the reality is that others will, most likely, be able to do certain job functions better than you can. Consider the 35-year-old entrepreneur who owns four local car washes. Most likely, his background does not include a previous accounting career. Although he may have managed his bookkeeping, budgeting, and tax filings for the first year of his business, a professional bookkeeper or accountant would be a valuable addition to his team as the business grows and expands.

3. **Service-Centric Model.** These types of businesses are really a combination of the customer-centric and economic-centric models with a twist. Most likely, they are businesses whose ability to capture and service customers is at their foundation, yet they've been able to integrate additional products or service offerings to increase the revenues generated by each customer. Typical businesses that fall into this category include:

- **Professional-Services Businesses** (resume-writing firm that offers career coaching, interview training, and other job-search services in partnership with other career providers and companies)

- **Technology-Consulting Firms** (hardware sales company that introduces a new line of software products and on-site installation/support services)

- **Retail Companies** (car dealership that adds a rental-car division; bookstore that adds an entire CD and video section)

- **Manufacturing Companies** (telecommunications products manufacturer that adds a service/installation division)

YOUR ENTREPRENEURIAL DECISIONS:
Business Type, Option and Model

Selecting Your Business Type

❑   Business Foundation: Core Professional Skills
     and Competencies
❑   Business Foundation: Personal Passion
❑   Business Foundation: Market, Economy and Industry
     Performance

Selecting Your Best Entrepreneurial Option

❑   Start Your Own Business From Scratch
❑   Buy an Established Business
❑   Join a Direct-Sales Company
❑   Purchase a Franchise
❑   Accept Equity Opportunity With Existing Business
❑   Succeed Into Family-Owned Business

Defining Your Business Model

❑   Customer-Centric
❑   Economic-Centric
❑   Service-Centric

MY BUSINESS WILL BE:

_____

_____

_____

_____

_____

_____

_____

_____

If the service-centric model is your preferred business model, then you need to pay special attention to the key issues and challenges of both customer-centric and economic-centric models. More specifically, you need to create a business that focuses on servicing, satisfying, and retaining your customer base, while letting go of some of the management and operating control that will be required as your business grows and expands.

Note that many service-centric businesses were originally launched as either a customer-centric or economic-centric entrepreneurial venture. Then, as these businesses grew, their owners realized that there were related business opportunities that they could capture. As such, over time, their businesses transitioned from one model to another to allow them the opportunity to continue to grow, diversify, and generate strong revenues and profits. Remember that the only constant in business is change!

Writing Your Business Plan

Now that you've devoted the time that is necessary to determine the right type of business and the right business model for your new venture, it's time to get down to the business at hand—writing your business plan. This initial step is, perhaps, the most important step in your entire business venture, for without a business plan, you have no direction and no course to follow.

Writing a business plan accomplishes several important things that are essential to each entrepreneur's immediate and long-term success:

- **The actual process of writing your business plan will allow you to get all of your ideas—the good ones and the bad ones—down on paper in a readable manner.** Once you've written it all down, you'll find that you'll immediately begin to make adjustments, changes, additions, deletions, and more. For example, it may be that your initial idea was to develop a management-consulting firm. However, after you've prepared the first draft of your business plan, you realize that a large percentage of the services that you'll be offering focus on human resources and workforce development. Instantly, you decide to change your business focus from general consulting to HR consulting to differentiate your firm from the thousands of other management-consulting firms.

- **The process of writing your plan also requires that you do all of the necessary research and obtain all of the necessary information that you'll need—today and in the near future.** For example, we recommend you include a section in your business plan about Competitive Market Forces. In order to accomplish this, you'll have to research your competition—who they are, what they offer, what they charge, and who their customers are. What's more, you'll want to research trends and projections about your specific market, industry, or profession. This information is tremendously valuable as you formulate your specific business strategies, operating procedures, pricing structures, and more.

- **Once your business plan is complete, you'll want to set up a schedule for reviewing it and updating it as time goes on.** In essence, your business plan is the map that you need to follow in order to accommodate all of the bends, turns, detours, and more that will, inevitably, block your way. Business ownership is a crooked road with lots of surprise turns, and you must be flexible in responding to those changes.

There is no magic formula for entrepreneurial success and, in fact, there are many variables that can impact your business performance—variables that you may have no control over (e.g., market conditions, economic conditions, competitive forces, customer preferences, new product and service offerings). In order to build a successful business, you must realize that your business plan is a living document that will constantly be changing in response to those demands. Realize that nothing you've written in your business plan is etched in stone and that it is the norm that your plan will constantly be changing as your venture moves forward, grows, diversifies, and expands.

The Core Ingredients of Successful Business Plans

Although business plans can be remarkably different in their writing, tone, style, and presentation, most plans share numerous common characteristics and common sections:

- Business Name, Mission Statement, and Vision Statement
- Executive Summary

- Legal Business Structure
- Regulatory, Licensing, and Permitting Requirements
- Operating Plan
- Financial Plan
- Marketing Plan
- Sales Plan
- Technology Requirements
- Equipment and Resource Requirements
- Board of Directors
- Key Personnel

Let's explore each of these key components in greater detail so that you'll understand the purpose of each section, the type of information to be included, and the important questions that your business plan must answer. You'll also find a list of resources at the end of this section where you can find detailed information, templates, and samples of business plans for use in developing your own plan.

Business Name, Mission, and Vision Statement

Purpose: A three-step process to clearly define "who" and "what" your business is, what it does, and what your long-term goals are.

Business Name: There are two distinct strategies for determining the name of your business. You can either select a name that clearly communicates the nature of the business (e.g., Toys 'R' Us) or choose a name that is more general in nature (e.g., Royce Management Consultants).

There are pros and cons to each of these choices. The name, Toys 'R' Us, tells you instantly what the company does. On the other hand, it does restrict the company in terms of the products it sells and the markets it reaches. On the other hand, a name such as Royce Management Consultants is vaguer. It's clear that the firm does management consulting, but that's a broad industry that does not immediately communicate the precise nature of the business. On the other hand, it does allow the business to diversify into new products, services, and market sectors while continuing to operate under the same name.

Key Questions to Ask Yourself:

- *What business name am I planning to use and why?*

- *Does my business name communicate what my business does?*

- *Does my business name allow for future change and diversification?*

- *If I'm planning to incorporate, is anyone else using that name?*

- *Has any other company registered or trademarked the business name I've selected? (If so, select a different name!)*

Mission Statement

A mission statement communicates a company's or organization's present goal and reason for being. For example, the mission statement of the National Conference (founded in 1927 as the National Conference of Christians and Jews) is:

> *A human relations organization dedicated to fighting bias, bigotry, and racism in America. The National Conference promotes understanding and acceptance of various religions and cultures through advocacy, conflict resolution, and education.*

Mission statements generally emerge during the initial strategic planning process when you're first developing your new venture.

Key Questions to Ask Yourself:

- *What are the opportunities or needs that my company will address? (This is more commonly referred to as the purpose of your organization.)*

- *How is my company going to address those needs? (This is more commonly referred to as the "business" of the organization.)*

- *What principles and beliefs will guide my company? (This is more commonly referred to as the values of the organization.)*

In order to be truly effective, your mission statement must:

- Express your company's purpose in a way that inspires support and ongoing commitment.

- Motivate everyone connected to your company.

- Be short enough that anyone connected to your company can easily repeat it.

- Use action-oriented verbs to describe what you do.

- Be articulated in a manner that is convincing and easy to grasp.

- Be free of industry-specific jargon.

Vision Statement

A vision statement communicates a company's or organization's vision for the future and its guiding image for long-term success. For example, the vision of United States Equestrian Federation is:

> ...to provide leadership for equestrian sport in the United States of America, promoting the pursuit of excellence from the grass roots to the Olympic Games, based on a foundation of fair, safe competition and the welfare of its human and equine athletes, and embracing this vision, to be the best national equestrian federation in the world.

Vision statements tend to be short, just one or two sentences, and are externally focused on communicating the value of a company to its intended audience. As such, a company's vision is often printed on business cards and advertisements, posted on a website, and otherwise widely publicized.

Key Questions to Ask Yourself:

- *What will success look like to me and my business?*

- *Is my vision statement realistic, credible, and focused on one common purpose?*

- *Can my vision statement be easily understood?*

- *Does my vision statement incorporate my beliefs?*

- *Is my vision statement appropriate, ambitious, and responsive to change?*

- *Will my vision statement challenge and inspire my business and my employees?*

Although writing a vision statement may seem to be an arduous and super-fluous task, don't overlook it! The long-term benefits can be substantial, for visioning will allow you to:

- Think beyond your normal boundaries.

- Identify business purpose and direction.

- Provide continuity and avoid the stutter effect of planning, re-planning, changing plans, etc.

- Promote interest in and commitment to your business.

- Encourage a laser-like focus.

- Open you to unique and creative solutions.

- Encourage confidence and build loyalty.

- Result in optimum efficiency and productivity within your organization.

Executive Summary

Purpose: To summarize the highlights and most relevant information from the major sections of your business plan. This is a particularly important component if you will be sharing your plan with others (e.g., investors, attorneys, accountants). Note that Executive Summaries are brief, generally only one to two pages in length.

Key Questions to Ask Yourself:

- *What is the most important information included in my business plan?*

- *How can I summarize those important components and briefly present them in a format that allows for a quick overview?*

- *How can I best present detailed financial, marketing, sales, and operating information from my business plan in just a few short paragraphs or bullet points?*

- *What language, tone, and writing style should I use to ensure that my Executive Summary is enticing to potential readers?*

- *What information should I include that will immediately communicate the viability and potential of my business for long-term success and financial reward?*

Legal Business Structure

Purpose: To define the legal structure of your entrepreneurial venture. Basically, you need to determine if you're going to establish your business as a corporation, limited liability corporation (LLC), self-proprietorship, or other entity.

Key Questions to Ask Yourself:

- *Do I know which legal structure is most appropriate for my venture and why?*

- *Do I need an attorney to help me set up my business and, if so, what type of attorney (e.g., general business, contracts, real estate, international)?*

- *What legal work, if any, can I do myself? (You'll be surprised how easy and inexpensive certain legal activities can be, such as registering your business in the state in which you plan to operate.)*

- *What type of insurance do I need and why (e.g., fire, theft, liability, workers' compensation, auto, errors and omissions)?*

- *How can I protect my business and my assets?*

To help you answer these questions and better understand the advantages and disadvantages of various legal structures, pay close attention to the table on pages 48-49 which outlines the plusses, minuses, and requirements of each of your options.

Regulatory, Licensing, and Permitting Requirements

Purpose: To ensure that your business is set up and operating in accordance with any federal, state, or local government requirements. These consist of local business licenses and permits, federal employee identification numbers, state sales tax numbers, state occupational licenses, federal licenses and permits, and special state and local regulatory requirements which vary from state to state and from community to community.

Legal Business Structure

Corporation:

Management	centralized management, board of directors, and corporate officers (maybe just you)
Capitalization	can issue stock for up to 35 outside shareholders
Owner's Liability	liability limited to assets in the corporation
Continuity of Life	indefinite life
Tax Year	calendar year OR Section 444 selection
Income Taxes	pass-through (see *www.irs.gov* for details)
Payroll	wage income paid to owners/employees; income, FICA and unemployment taxes withheld; quarterly estimated tax payments

LLC:

Management	typically controlled by an operating agreement
Capitalization	sources of capital expand by virtue of number of partners involved
Owner's Liability	investor's liability—often limited
Continuity of Life	generally limited
Tax Year	Section 444 selection
Income Taxes	pass-through (see *www.irs.gov* for details)
Payroll	pass-through income; quarterly estimated tax payments

Proprietorship:

Management	single owner—characterized by simplicity, flexibility, and control
Capitalization	limited to owner's assets and loans
Owner's Liability	unlimited liability
Continuity of Life	finite life—ceases upon the death of the proprieter
Tax Year	generally, the calendar year
Income Taxes	pass-through (see *www.irs.gov* for details)
Payroll	self-employment earnings; pay FICA and income tax quarterly estimates

Key Questions to Ask Yourself:

- *What federal government requirements must I meet?*
- *What state government requirements must I meet?*
- *What local government requirements must I meet?*
- *Do I need an attorney or accountant to assist me in preparing and filing these documents?*
- *Are these activities I need to engage in only at the start of my business or are there annual filing and compliance requirements?*

Operating Plan

Purpose: To create a working plan—a blueprint—that outlines the day-to-day operations of your business. This is one of the most critical and most detailed sections of your business plan, and should encompass all facets of your operation. In fact, this section is your roadmap to guide you in establishing and then managing each and every function within your organization.

Note that the following list of questions to be answered is extensive. Some of these will be pertinent to you and your business, while others may not, depending on your specific entrepreneurial venture.

Key Questions to Ask Yourself:

- *Location: What is the best location for my business? Do I need a storefront operation, office, factory, warehouse, or other type of facility, or can I operate from my home? What is the most convenient and cost-effective location for my targeted customer base? "Location is everything" best summarizes the success of many businesses (McDonald's and Wal-Mart which are both well noted for their attention to location).*

- *Staffing: Do I need any employees to start my business? If so, how many and what functions will they be responsible for? What are my projected staffing needs as my business grows? What type of personnel will I need and what will they do? Should I hire full-time or part-time employees, temporary personnel, or contractors? How can I best recruit to find qualified individuals? Should I use the Internet, classified advertisements, employment firms, headhunters, or networking? How do I plan to pay my personnel—hourly wage, annual salary, commission, bonus, or a combination?*

- *Materials: What materials, supplies, equipment, technology, furnishings, telecommunication systems, or other things do I need to purchase to start my business? What will I need to purchase on a regular basis to maintain my ongoing operations? Who are the best vendors for me to work with and how do I find them? What payment terms and credit arrangements should I negotiate? What inventory control and reporting system am I going to use? Do I need to create an entire logistics and supply-chain management function?*

- *Operations: How is my business going to work on a daily basis? What are my operating plans, policies, and procedures? What can I do to ensure optimum efficiency and productivity? What quality standards am I going to put into place? What specific operating systems will I put in place? How am I going to manufacture my products, deliver my services, sell my merchandise, or transport my passengers?*

Financial Plan

Purpose: To present critical information about the financial requirements for the start-up and continued operation of your business, along with charts, graphs, or spreadsheets of your projected financial performance. This should likely include projected costs (operating and capital budgets), revenues, market-share ratings, and profits. For potential investors, this section of your business plan is by far the most important. Therefore, be certain that you include as much information as possible . . . information, facts, and figures that are detailed, accurate, and, hopefully, positive.

Key Questions to Ask Yourself:

- *How can I best finance the start-up of my business and its ongoing operation?*

- *Should I use my own savings? Take out a personal or business loan with a bank? Get a loan from the Small Business Administration? Secure private investor financing?*

- *How much financing do I need to ensure that I'm not under-capitalized and poised for immediate failure because of over-spending on rent, furnishings, inventory, personnel, advertising, or other business expenses?*

- *What are my monthly operating costs for the first year (including initial start-up costs)?*

- *What are my monthly operating costs once my business is established?*

- *At what percentage will my operating costs increase as my business grows and expands?*

- *What are my projected revenues and from what markets or customers are they generated?*

- *At what rate do I forecast my revenues increasing?*

- *When do I anticipate breaking even with my new venture?*

- *When do I anticipate showing a profit?*

- *What accounting system should I use—cash or accrual?*

- *Can I handle the books myself or do I need to hire a part-time bookkeeper or full-time accountant? What about quarterly and annual financial statements and tax returns?*

- *What type of savings plan (e.g., IRA, CDs, money market account) will I be starting as soon as I can?*

Marketing Plan

Purpose: To define who your customers are, where they are, what they want, and how to capture them through an intense market research effort. Just as important, your marketing plan will include critical information about your marketing message and how you plan to communicate that message.

Key Questions to Ask Yourself:

- *Where is my market—local, regional, national, or international?*
- *Who are my customers and what products/services am I going to provide to them?*
- *What companies will I be competing with? What do they do, what do they charge, how do they market their services, where do they advertise, and who are their customers?*
- *Are there other competitive forces or external factors that I discovered through my market research?*
- *How can I best position my company within my targeted market?*
- *What is my marketing message?*
- *What marketing channels am I going to use to communicate my message?*
- *Who is going to develop my brochures, website, product literature, advertisements, promotional material, and other marketing communications?*

Sales Plan

Purpose: To define how you will transition your marketing plan from theory into action. Specifically, your sales plan is the step-by-step process for how you plan to capture your customers, sell your products or services, manage your customer-service operations, and retain your customer base. Bottom-line, your sales plan states how you plan to make money and that's what entrepreneurship is all about.

Key Questions to Ask Yourself:

- *How can I reach out and capture my customers?*

- *What selling strategies will I use?*

- *Are my sales presentation, negotiation, and closing skills strong?*

- *Should I develop special sales promotions and incentives?*

- *What specific sales channels (e.g., retail, direct sales, website, Internet advertising, mail order, business-to-business) am I going to use and how much business do I expect to generate from each channel?*

- *How can I develop a "best-in-class" customer-service operation?*

- *How can I survey my customers to get their feedback for improving my products and/or services?*

- *What will I do to retain my existing customer base while continuing to seek out new customers and new opportunities?*

Technology Requirements

Purpose: To identify and define your specific computer, telecommunications, and other technology systems requirements in order to build and sustain your business operations. In today's world, where so much business is conducted and/or managed via technology, it is critical that you know what systems you need and why.

Key Questions to Ask Yourself:

- *What computer and telecommunications systems do I need?*

- *Do I have other technology requirements based on my particular business?*

- *Is it better to buy or lease my systems?*

- *What are the best sources for acquiring those systems?*

- *Where can I get help in identifying what I need and then learning how to operate/manage these systems?*

- *Do I need to be on the leading edge of technology or can I acquire systems that are more commonplace, yet meet my needs?*

- *What changes in my technology requirements do I anticipate as my business grows, expands, and diversifies?*

Equipment and Resource Requirements

Purpose: To identify and define your equipment requirements beyond your basic computer and telecommunications needs. This will be particularly relevant to certain types of businesses (e.g., manufacturing, warehousing, automotive, technical services, building trades, maritime, aviation).

Key Questions to Ask Yourself:

- *Do I have equipment requirements beyond basic computer and telecommunications systems?*
- *What are my specific equipment needs and for what purpose?*
- *Where are the best resources to acquire this equipment?*
- *Will my equipment needs change as my business expands?*
- *Do I need expert advice to guide me during my equipment acquisition process?*
- *Is it best to purchase or lease this equipment?*
- *Do I need to be on the leading edge of technology or can I acquire systems that are more commonplace, yet meet my needs?*

Board of Directors

Purpose: To assemble a team of experts to help you with business planning, strategic planning, networking, business development, financing, operations, and more. It's always wise to include respected individuals who can contribute their particular expertise and perspective to your business.

Key Questions to Ask Yourself:

- *Do I need a Board of Directors or Board of Advisors?*
- *Do I plan to compensate my Board members and, if so, how?*
- *Have I selected Board members who each bring a different area of expertise to my company?*
- *Where can I find these individuals and how do I approach them to ask for their participation?*

- *How often should I meet with my Board and should I meet with them individually or as a group?*

- *What type of information will I need to present to my Board to keep them apprised of the specific operations, financial performance, and challenges of my business?*

Key Personnel

Purpose: To identify the key management team and personnel for your venture, and include detailed information about their specific background and capabilities. This section of your business plan is generally quick and easy to assemble; in fact, I recommend that you include professional resumes or biographies for yourself and any other key personnel within the company.

Key Questions to Ask Yourself:

- *Am I the only principal in the company or do I have other partners?*

- *Have I already recruited an individual or several individuals to join my organization?*

- *Have I clearly communicated the value, knowledge, and expertise that I bring to the company?*

- *Have I clearly communicated the value, knowledge, and expertise that others bring to my organization?*

- *Does this section present a picture of either an individual or a team of professionals who are well qualified to build and manage my entrepreneurial venture?*

Business Plan Tools, Resources, and Templates

Following are some of my favorite business plan resources—some that are free and others that are not. They are listed alphabetically, in no order of preference. I strongly recommend that you review several of these websites and tools to obtain as much information as you can before you begin writing your own business plan. Then, if you're still struggling, you may consider working with a professional writer having expertise in business plan development.

- *www.allbusiness.com*
- *www.bplans.com*
- *www.businessplanarchive.org*
- *www.businessplanpro.com*
- *www.businessplans.com*
- *www.businessplans.org*
- *www.businessweek.com*
- *www.business-plan-success.com*
- *www.entremate.com*
- *www.growthink.com*
- *www.loc.gov/rr/business/assists/busplans.html*
- *www.masterplans.com*
- *www.morebusiness.com*
- *www.mybusinessanalyst.com*
- *www.planware.org*
- *www.score.org/template_gallery.html*
- *www.iedtexas.org/sbdcnet/*
- *www.smallbusiness.net*
- *www.thebeehive.org*
- *www.zbusinessplans.com*

4 Building Your Empire:
Sales, Marketing, Branding, Advertising, and More

L ET'S FACE IT...NO MATTER HOW miraculous your product or how phenomenal your service, if you can't market and sell it, it simply doesn't matter. Your business will only be as successful as your ability to build your customer base, close sales, deliver your products or services, and generate revenues. Bottom-line, making money is what it's all about (or, at least, what most of it is about)!

Unfortunately, this is where all too many entrepreneurs often fail. They are under the impression that their product or service is so wonderful that it will simply sell itself. Be realistic and know that will never happen!

Suppose you've designed, patented, and manufactured the most innovative new lawn sprinkler ever to hit the market. Or, perhaps you've developed a new technology solution that will revolutionize the entire database management industry. If you don't have strong marketing and advertising programs in place, a clear brand message, and effective sales strategies, no one will ever know. And, if they don't know, it won't sell and you won't make any money. It's that simple.

That's why this chapter is so important to both the immediate and long-term success of your business. Read it carefully and know that a huge amount of your time and effort will be dedicated to building your sales and marketing organization, creating your sales and marketing materials, designing print and online advertisements, creating innovative promotions, and managing the client-sales process. Every successful entrepreneur must also be a strategic marketer, powerful sales representative, shrewd advertising specialist, and more!

What is Business Development?

Before we can even begin to start talking about the specifics of sales, marketing, and related business-development functions, it's critical that we define some of the most important words and concepts related to these functions.

- **Advertising:** Paid, informative, and persuasive messages communicated to your target customers through various print, broadcast, electronic, and online media channels. Designed to positively influence the purchasing behavior and/or thought patterns of your target audience.

- **Brand:** Identifying mark, symbol, word(s), or combination thereof that separates one company's products and services from another. Your brand provides your company with its unique position within the marketplace.

- **Marketing:** Activities and programs associated with promoting products and services for sale. Classic components are the 4 P's: product, price, place, and promotion.

- **Promotions:** Activities, materials, devices, and techniques used to supplement advertising and marketing efforts (e.g., sweepstakes, coupons, special displays, promotional discounts, contests, gift offers). Often referred to as sales promotions since they are generally offered in cooperation with more traditional sales programs.

- **Public Relations:** Special form of communication that is primarily designed to build a company's image and that often deals with issues rather than specific products or services. Public relations campaigns use free publicity in a variety of media channels and are often placed as news or items of public interest.

- **Sales:** The exchange of money for products and/or services.

Key Business-Development Concepts

Following are my top five strategies for success in business development—today, tomorrow, and for years to come. Most, if not all of these, will be applicable to your entrepreneurial venture, no matter your particular line of business.

1. **Customer Capture:** We've all heard the old adage that you don't want to sell to your customers. Rather, you want your customers to choose to buy from you because you have a great product or service, a well-known and recognizable brand, and/or a strong reputation in the marketplace. Customer capture is a tremendously important concept that you must give careful thought and attention to, for it will serve as the foundation for your entire sales, marketing, and business-development function.

2. **Consistency:** The key to all your marketing, advertising, public relations, and promotional efforts is consistency in brand, image, marketing message, and sales process. Think about the Nike swoosh and the fact that every time you see a Nike advertisement—online, in print, or on television—the visual image and brand is always the same. It's the same on their marketing literature, product promotions, advertisements, and press releases. The swoosh is Nike—at least in the consumer's mind.

3. **Likability:** People want to do business with people whom they like. It's that simple. Think about how good you feel when you walk into your local drugstore and the pharmacist knows your name and asks how your day has been. You're not just doing business there to get a prescription; rather, you're enjoying the customer experience, recognition, and personal touch. This concept extends far beyond your local retail establishment and can be just as important if you're a much larger organization. Consider when you call American Airlines and you actually get a reservations agent who is friendly and responsive to your needs. You're delightfully surprised and will long remember that exchange and personal connection.

4. **Personal Relationships:** In an online world, you have to work a bit harder to reach out to your customers and create

a personal relationship. If you service your customer base on an entirely electronic platform, where there is no person-to-person or telephone interaction, you must implement other actionable programs that allow you to *touch* and *feel* your customers. Your challenge is to create the perception that each interaction is an *individual* interaction.

5. **Networking:** This should be a key component of every company's business-development efforts. Frankly, there is no better way to promote your company, your products, and/or your services than through one-on-one interaction with others. Work to build your professional network by affiliating with professional associations, business groups, Chambers of Commerce, university-alumni groups, colleagues, and others in your business or industry. Then work to develop your personal network of contacts that can be built and nurtured through your involvement in charitable, volunteer, religious, school-based, and other organizations.

6. **Customer Care:** Let your customers know that you value them, their business, and their loyalty to your company. Everyone wants to be appreciated and your customers are no different. After you've worked so hard to capture them through your various marketing, advertising, and sales efforts, you have to work to keep them. Always remember that customer relationship management and retention are just as vital to your success as the initial customer capture!

Marketing

The classic components of marketing are often referred to as the 4 P's:

- **Product:** selection and development of your product (or service)
- **Price:** determination of product (or service) pricing
- **Place:** selection and design of distribution and advertising channels (how to get the message out)
- **Promotion:** generating a demand for the product

These 4 P's should be the foundation for your entire marketing function. Each time you have a new product or service to bring to the market, a next-generation product or service, or a new product or service enhancement or feature, you'll follow these four principles to guide the development of your specific marketing initiatives.

For example, if you've designed a new kitchen appliance, you'll set its pricing based on cost, value, and the pricing of competitive products. You'll then determine how to place it into the market to create customer demand through multi-faceted advertising, promotional, and sales campaigns. This is the process you should follow each and every time.

Other critical concepts and activities that are core functions within an effective and successful marketing discipline include the following. Each of these should become key components of your own marketing efforts:

- **Market Research:** Investigation and analysis of the size, characteristics, demographics, and potential of a market to determine what customers want and need. Market research is normally done in advance of a new product or service development initiative, and encompasses all marketing activities from product/service concept through final launch. I cannot stress enough how important your market-research efforts will be to the long-term success of your marketing and sales programs. You must clearly identify if, and where, a potential market exists. If there is none, it is certainly not worth your time, effort, or investment to create new products and services where there is no demand.

- **Market Segmentation:** Process of dividing a market according to similar characteristics and/or needs that exist among the various subgroups within the market. These subgroups can be based on age, race, ethnicity, socio-economic status, interests, occupations, and much more. Once your markets are segmented, you can then customize your marketing messages to meet the specific needs and expectations of each targeted group.

- **Market Share:** Percentage of industry-wide sales of a specific company, product, or service. This statistical information is invaluable in further developing your products, services, and marketing plans in order to keep pace (ideally, outpace) your competition.

- **Market Test:** Exposure of products or services to a small sample of the entire market to test and evaluate customer response to the product and to various marketing strategies. Market testing can yield tremendously valuable results that will help you further define and build new products and services that meet future market demands and customer expectations.

- **Market Mix:** Combination of marketing elements used in the sale of a particular product or service. This may include print literature about your products and services, online product and service information, brand development, promotions, public-relations initiatives, and other programs designed to bring visibility to your company.

- **Market Plan:** Detailed plan that outlines a company's specific market program and effort. Can be developed for the entire company or a particular product/service line. Your marketing plan may be the most important marketing effort of all because it details what you're going to market, to whom, and how. The following are very important items that are key to your marketing plan and will lay the foundation for what marketing initiatives you launch, where, when, and how. Bottom-line, the goal of your marketing plan is to:

  - **Define your product or service** offerings.

  - **Define your target market(s)**—local, regional, national, or international; retail, professional, industrial, institutional, or government. (Note that these are often referred to as your niche markets.)

  - **Define your target customers**—B2C (business-to-consumer) or B2B (business-to-business).

  - **Create your marketing message**, which may differ from one product to another, one service to another, one market to another, or one customer base to another.

  - **Identify the step-by-step actions** to advertise and promote your product to your various target markets and customer bases.

  - **Create a step-by-step sales process** that may vary from one product to another, one service to another, one market to another, or one customer base to another.

Marketing should always come before product development, promotions, and sales. In fact, your marketing plan will drive the development of all of your other business-development plans and activities.

Knowing that, you must also understand that it is critical that you find time to devote to marketing…now…today. Developing your marketing plan, writing your marketing messages, and implementing your marketing programs take time to do and time to deliver results. If you wait until the last minute to do these activities, you'll be too late and find yourself sitting alone in your office for months and months waiting for your marketing efforts to take effect. Do these things in advance, while you're building the other components of your business. Then, when everything else is in place, your marketing will have kicked in and the rest will be history!

Newsletters as Marketing Tools

One of the most powerful marketing tools for the small-business entre-preneur is the client newsletter. In simple terms, a newsletter is a tool that allows you to quickly, easily, and inexpensively communicate with your customers. You can introduce new products and services, announce an up-coming public-speaking engagement, highlight special promotions, provide interesting information about your industry, welcome a new employee, and so much more.

In more complex terms, newsletters provide you with a platform to:

- Strengthen your market penetration
- Stay in touch with your customers (so they're sure to become repeat customers)
- Reach out to new customers (prospecting)
- Strengthen your brand (you'll read more about branding later in this chapter)
- Position yourself as an expert in your specific industry or profession (people always want to do business with experts)
- Build your credibility and market visibility
- Distinguish yourself from your competition
- Outpace your competition

What's more, producing newsletters is easy! In years past, before the emer-gence of many of today's technologies, newsletters were generally transmitted via postal mail. Today, however, you can quickly produce newsletters using electronic tools for writing, design, and distribution, slashing your costs and expediting production and delivery.

Whether you decide to produce the more traditional print newsletter or an electronic newsletter, here are some excellent online tools that provide a wealth of information about writing and producing newsletters that your customers will want to read:

- *http://clickz.com* (Newsletter for online marketers)
- *http://directmag.com* (Direct-marketing and list-management newsletters)
- *http://emailuniverse.com* (Newsletter on email newsletters)
- *www.azobleassoc.com* ("Do-able" marketing newsletter)
- *www.constantcontact.com* (Email marketing hints and tips newsletter)
- *www.EasyEzineToolkit.com* (Online newsletter toolkit)
- *www.eMarketer.com* (Internet marketing and e-commerce newsletter)
- *www.greatestnetworker.com* (Network-marketing forums and newsletter)
- *www.howtowriteanewsletter.com* (Newsletter tutorial)
- *www.ideasiteforbusiness.com* (Marketing ideas newsletter)
- *www.marketingtips.com* (Marketing newsletter)
- *www.twipress.com* (Direct-marketing copywriting newsletter)

Newsletters work best when they're produced on a regularly scheduled basis. In fact, over time, your customers will start to anticipate the arrival of your newsletter and the valuable information that you provide. So, whether you decide to produce your newsletter on a monthly basis, a quarterly basis, or some other schedule, be sure that you are consistent.

All too many entrepreneurs start off with grand expectations that they'll deliver a visually impressive and content-rich newsletter each and every month. Then, after just a few months, they become overwhelmed with other responsibilities and their newsletter simply falls off the radar. To avoid this potential pitfall, make your newsletter easy to produce and don't over-commit yourself to a schedule that will be impossible to keep up.

Create a Powerful Visual Image

Often people don't meet you; instead, they meet a piece of paper, a website, or a business card. Therefore, it is critical that the visual presentation and content of these visual components of your business be the very best that they can be. Invest in sharp-looking, upscale business cards and brochures. In fact, invest in a graphic artist who can design an image that is unique and reflects you and your business. Prospective clients and business colleagues may not remember meeting you, no matter how positive the impression that you make. The only thing those clients will have to remember you is your business card or brochure, so be sure they communicate a strong and memorable impression.

Invest in a graphic artist who can design an image that reflects you and your business.

Then, take it one step further and translate that same design to your website to ensure that all of your marketing communications are consistent and present the same image and high degree of professionalism. Unless you happen to be a web designer, we strongly urge you to hire an expert who can effectively translate a print message into an electronic message that communicates the same look and feel, and same level of professionalism.

A great resource for developing logos, website templates, and more is *www.templatemonster.com*.

Branding

What is a brand? Simply put, it is an identifying mark, symbol, word(s), or combination thereof that distinguishes one company's products and services from another. Your brand should clearly communicate what makes your company different, special, compelling, and memorable, which, in turn, will give you a unique position within the marketplace. In essence, your brand defines your market identity.

The concept of branding has been around for decades. Just think about all of the consumer products that you purchase at the grocery store each week. Most of them will have well-known brand recognition (Tetley, Charmin, Stouffer's, Pepperidge Farm, Heinz) which allows these companies to separate themselves from their competitors. In turn, this increases their market visibility, sales revenues, and, hopefully, their bottom-line profitability.

Many brands, in and of themselves, communicate a specific message to their target markets and customers. Consider these well-known brands:

- **Harley Davidson** (It's an experience, not a motorcycle)
- **Volvo** (Promise of safety and security)
- **Starbucks** (Lifestyle choice; refuge away from home and work)
- **Disney** (Premier brand of family entertainment)

Perhaps one of the greatest branding stories today is that of Google. Just a few years ago, Google didn't even exist. Now, not only is it a premier Internet search engine and an experience, it's also a widely used verb ("I googled for a restaurant in that area."). You can't do any better with your branding than the people at Google!

There are a wealth of benefits that can be enjoyed through strategic and effective branding:

- Increased market visibility
- Unique position within the market
- Differentiation from your peers and your competitors
- Justification for increasing your prices and fees
- Justification for growth and expansion
- Ability to thrive in a downward economy
- Increased entrepreneurial confidence that comes with success

What's more, once your brand is clearly defined, it provides you with a direction for continued business development and keeps you focused on how you deliver value to your clients. In turn, you'll operate from a position of power and be well poised to meet your business operating and financial goals.

Now that you understand what a brand is and its value to your company, let's explore several other important and related concepts:

- **Brand Image:** Qualities that customers associate with a specific brand, expressed in terms of human behavior, desires, and perceptions, but that also relate to price, quality, and use of the brand. This image is not part of the brand name, but is created through advertising.
- **Brand Loyalty:** Degree to which a consumer will repeatedly purchase the same brand. Brand loyalty is driven by the consumer's perception that the brand offers the right combination of quality and price.

- **Brand Name:** Part of a brand or trademark that can be spoken and is distinguishable from any identifying symbol. Brand names usually consist of a word, letter, or group of words or letters.

- **Trademark:** Logo, design, picture, number, word, letter, or other graphic representation that distinguishes one company's goods or services from another. Remember the Nike swoosh!

Branding Resources

The following online and print resources will help you develop your unique branding focus:

Branding Websites:

- *www.brandchannel.com*
- *www.fastcompany.com*
- *www.petermontoya.com*
- *www.reachcc.com*
- *www.sethgodin.com*
- *www.tompeters.com*

Branding Blogs:

- *http://800ceoread.com/blog*
- *http://blog.guykawasaki.com*
- *http://blog.williamarruda.com*
- *www.careerhub.typepad.com*
- *www.innovationtools.com/weblog/weblog_chrono.asp*

Branding Books:

- *All Marketers are Liars: The Power of Telling Authentic Stories in a Low-Trust World* (Seth Godin)
- *Be Your Own Brand* (David McNally and Karl D. Speak)
- *Get Slightly Famous: Become a Celebrity in Your Field and Attract More Business with Less Effort* (Steven Van Yoder)

- *A Whole New Mind: Moving from the Information Age to the Conceptual Age* (Daniel Pink)
- *The Personal Branding Phenomenon* (Peter Montoya)
- *The Potato Chip Difference* (Michael Goodman)
- *Purple Cow* (Seth Godin)

Use the form on pages 69-71 for identifying your own unique brand.

Sales

Enough of the tedious discussion about business development, marketing plans, marketing mix, market share, brand development, and more. Now it's time for the fun part! And, yes, sales is the fun part. It's the actionable component of all of your marketing and branding efforts; the component that generates revenues and puts money in your pocket.

To start exploring the critical business function of sales, let's begin with some of the most important basics:

Three Categories of Sales Connections

There are three primary ways to sell your products and services:

- Person-to-person sales
- Telephone sales
- Invisible sales (website sales)

How you sell to your customers will depend entirely on the type of business you own, the products and services that you sell, your market reach, your customer base, and your pricing structure. Consider the different selling strategies used in these three unique interactions:

- John is the owner and operator of TC Solutions in Toledo, Ohio. He works primarily with small-business owners to design, install, and support telecommunications and networking systems. His projects range in cost from $1,000 to $10,000, depending on each company's specific technology needs. John meets individually with clients, usually on several occasions, to identify their needs, present his proposal, negotiate pricing, and close the sale. This is a perfect example of #1—**person-to-person sales.**

Identifying Your Unique Brand

Use this worksheet to identify the unique brand of your company and then create your branding statement.

Step #1: Answer the following questions with as much detail as possible:

1. What are the **core strengths, skills, and competencies** of your company, your products, and/or your services?

_____

_____

_____

_____

_____

_____

_____

_____

_____

2. What makes your company, products, and/or services **unique and distinguishable** from your competition?

_____

_____

_____

_____

_____

_____

_____

_____

3. What **messages** do you want to communicate about your company, your products, and/or your services?

_____

_____

_____

_____

_____

_____

_____

_____

_____

4. Who is your **target audience** and what are their needs?

_____

_____

_____

_____

_____

_____

_____

_____

_____

5. How do you **deliver value** to your target markets and target customers?

_____

_____

_____

_____

_____

_____

_____

_____

Step #2: Select the **words, concepts, and ideas** from your answers to items 1-5 above that you want to communicate to your customers and be certain to integrate into your branding statement.

_____

_____

_____

_____

_____

_____

_____

_____

_____

Step #3: Draft your **branding statement** from your notes in Step #2.

_____

_____

_____

_____

_____

_____

_____

_____

_____

_____

_____

_____

_____

_____

_____

_____

_____

_____

_____

- Dolores founded a specialty-arts business that sells to collectors nationwide from her ranch in Wyoming. Her customers hear about her almost exclusively through word-of-mouth referrals from her past customers, other collectors, upscale galleries, and museums. Prospective customers contact her via phone, she mails photographs of her art, and then they call back to place telephone orders. She rarely meets a client in person; more than 90% of her business is transacted over the phone. This is a perfect example of #2—**telephone sales.**

- Margaret recently established a website to sell her own brand of pastries to the general public. Her website hosts a complete product catalog and a sophisticated e-commerce capability that allows her clients to process their orders online with no direct communication with her. They visit the site, click on their product preferences, enter their credit card information, and the transaction is completed. This is a perfect example of #3—**invisible sales.**

Earlier we presented the concept that people want to do business with people whom they like and that's never more true than when we're talking about sales. And it's particularly true when we're discussing the one-on-one selling relationship between you, the business owner and sales representative of your company, and your customer. Build relationships and you'll benefit with strong sales revenues and strong bottom-line profits!

Take the time that is necessary to get to know each client and listen carefully to what they have to say. Then, leverage that information to your advantage by customizing your sales presentations to their wants, their needs, and their expectations.

Three Customer Types

- New Customers
- Repeat Customers
- Referred Customers

All customers are good customers—generally! However, consider the fact that every time you capture a *new* customer, it costs money. Advertising generates new customers and advertising costs money. It's that simple.

For detailed information, refer to the Client-Capture Analysis Formula in Chapter 6, *Money: Does It Grow on Your Tree?*

Now, consider the fact that there is no cost of capture associated with servicing repeat customers or getting referrals, and you'll understand why it is so important that you build a strong and sustainable customer-service and relationship-management function. You can read much more about the critical functions of customer service and client relations in Chapter 5, *Customers, Clients and Patrons: Can't Live With Them; Can't Live Without Them!*

Top-10 Selling Tips

The following selling tips will help you build your business one customer at a time:

1. **Don't be shy about asking for referrals!** Those who ask, will receive. Referrals are the key to building a successful and profitable business.

2. **Learn to sell it, not just tell it!** Whether you're selling in person, on the phone, or online, truly successful salespeople know that selling a product (emphasizing benefits) is a remarkably more effective strategy than simply telling a customer about a product (its features).

3. **Be accessible to your customers** or, at a minimum, have someone else who's accessible. How often have you called a business and no one answered? What did you do then? Most likely, you called another business! If your customers can't get to you, they will go elsewhere.

4. **Teach your clients rather than try to hard-sell them.** Indeed, some of the best salespeople are former teachers. They help educate clients as to the value of their product or service. In doing so, they become authentic and trustworthy.

5. **Listen to your customers!** *"Good listeners generally make more sales than good talkers"* (Anonymous). Listen to what your customers have to say—about your business, your products, your services, your responsiveness, your quality . . . anything and everything. It's remarkably valuable information that can drive significant improvements in your operations and your profitability.

6. **Learn your customers' buying signals.** What do your customers respond to? Certain kinds of advertisements? Special promotions and coupon mailers? Upscale, high-impact product literature? Distinguishing professional credentials? Industry honors and awards? The list is endless. It's your responsibility to discover—over time—what makes your customers buy from you. Then, use that information to further customize your marketing messages and sales efforts to strengthen your market position and revenue performance.

7. **Be sure to capture names and contact information** everywhere you go. Whether you're attending a local Chamber event, speaking at a professional conference, participating in a networking event, or any one of a score of other professional activities, be sure to get business cards from everyone. You never know whom you'll meet and what potential synergies may exist between your business and their needs. Don't ever make the assumption that the people you meet at a particular event are not your potential customers. You never know who or what they know!

8. **Don't be shy about handing out your business cards**—to everyone and anyone! There is no shame in self-promotion, particularly for entrepreneurs. Visibility, recognition, and acknowledgment are critical, particularly if you're selling to customers within your local region.

9. **Explore the potential for unique and cooperative selling relationships.** More often than not, a sale is between your company and your customer. However, more and more firms are now leveraging their joint resources and engaging in strategic alliances, co-marketing agreements, joint ventures, and other types of partnerships and alliances. Why? Because they allow you to extend your reach into new markets, penetrate new customer bases, leverage the sales teams of both organizations, deliver bundled solutions and services, and, in the long run, drive revenue growth for both companies. These are powerful relationships that have significant potential and are definitely worth investigating if you think they may be reasonable courses of action for you.

10. **Even if all of your business is online, write and design a print brochure** (or other sales and product/service literature) that

you can mail or email to prospective clients so they can *touch* and *feel* you. Instantly, you become real and not just some vague, online entity. This is a great way to capture clients, build one-on-one client relationships, and outperform your competition.

One very important note . . . you're not going to sell everyone and that's okay! This can be an extremely difficult lesson to learn, but not everyone is going to think that your products or services are the best (although, of course, they are!). Sometimes, it just doesn't work out. Learn to let it go and move on to the next customer, and your entire life will be better!

Advertising

Let's start at the beginning with a clear definition of what advertising is:

Paid, informative, and persuasive messages communicated to your target customers through various print, broadcast, electronic, and online media channels. Effective advertisements are designed to positively influence the purchasing behavior and/or thought patterns of your target audience.

With that definition in mind, you can then understand that the type of advertising program you develop and the messages that those ads communicate will depend entirely on the target markets and target customers that you are trying to reach.

As a baseline for writing and designing your advertisements, ask yourself these three critical questions:

- **Who are my customers?** What demographic groups? What do they share in common? What markets do they represent?

- **How can I reach them?** What print publications—newspapers, journals, and magazines—do they read? What television stations do they watch? What radio stations do they listen to? What online sites do they frequent?

- **What important messages must I communicate** to them to entice them to purchase my product or service?

To develop truly effective advertising campaigns, I recommend that you call in the experts. A graphic designer, advertising specialist, copywriter, and website designer can be valuable additions to your team while providing the expertise that you may lack.

A word of caution . . . be careful not to over-spend. Many start-up entrepreneurs are so eager to get the message out, that they over-commit on their advertising budgets. This can be a critical and very costly mistake. Don't let it happen to you!

Press Relations and Public Relations

Press relations and public relations focus on external communications with various media outlets, special-interest groups, professional associations, targeted customer audiences, and the general public. They are primarily designed to build and strengthen a company's image within the market and, as such, often focus on issues rather than a company's specific products or services.

One of the most common forms of press outreach and public relations is the press release, distributed throughout multiple media channels and professional communities, and often placed as news or items of public interest. These efforts can often yield remarkable results, ranging from a small business announcement in your local newspaper to a full-blown article in a national press outlet. And it's free!

Here are five essential tips that will help you to write effective press releases and work the media to your advantage.

- **Wait for slow news days** (e.g., celebratory holidays, government holidays) to send your press release. Reporters are often scrambling for news on those days, so you're much more likely to capture someone's attention and get coverage.

- **Be unusual.** News covers the abnormal and not the mundane. Give the press something interesting, new, exciting, different, or unique.

- **Be visual.** Reporters use pictures to tell stories, so create media events that have great supporting visuals. For example, if you own a meeting-planning company, use photographs from your most visually impressive event to accompany your story.

- **Write like a reporter.** If you're writing a press release, use a heading that would be similar to what you'd see in a newspaper or on television; then make the rest of your story more conversational in tone so that a reporter could simply use it as is. If you do this, you will make the reporter's job much easier and significantly increase your chances of getting positive news coverage.

- **Identify the right reporter.** Almost every media outlet has a website that will list the key personnel within their organization (e.g., business editor, lifestyle editor, finance editor). Your chances for positive response are much better if you send your press release to the *right* person and department.

Be sure to check out *www.PRWeb.com*, an affordable press-release distribution service. There are numerous other companies offering similar services, and a quick Google search will identify them all for you.

On page 80 you'll find a sample press release that you can use as the foundation for writing your own releases.

Great Resources for Sales, Marketing, and Business Development

Books:

- *101 Ways to Boost Your Web Traffic* (Thomas Wong)
- *Authentic Leadership: Courage in Action* (Dr. Robert Terry)
- *Creating You & Company* (William Bridges)
- *E-Newsletters That Work: The Small Business Owner's Guide* (Michael J. Katz)
- *Guerrilla Marketing Secrets for Making Big Profits from Your Small Business* (Jay Conrad Levinson)
- *Guerrilla PR: How to Wage an Effective Publicity Campaign* (Michael Levine)
- *How to Become a Rainmaker* (Jeffrey J. Fox)
- *Jump Start Your Business Brain: Win More, Lose Less & Make More Money* (Doug Hall)
- *Multiple Streams of Income* (Robert Allen)
- *Net Results: Web Marketing That Works* (Rick Bruner)
- *Networds: Creating High-Impact Online Copy* (Nick Usbourne)
- *Nichecraft: Using Your Specialness to Focus Your Business, Corner Your Market, and Make Customers Seek You Out* (Dr. Lynda Falkenstein)

- *Permission-Based E-Mail Marketing That Works!* (Kim MacPherson)

- *Publicity on the Internet* (Steve O'Keefe)

- *Selling the Invisible* (Harry Beckwith)

- *The Online Copywriter's Handbook* (Robert W. Bly)

Websites:

- *http://bly.com* (Bob Bly's copywriting wisdom)

- *http://www.dmnews.com* (Internet marketing and direct marketing news)

- *www.bizjournals.com* ("News agent" for local business articles)

- *www.constantcontact.com* (Email marketing hints and tips newsletter)

- *www.econtentmag.com* (e-content technology, tools and trends)

- *www.MarketingSherpa.com* (Marketing news, case studies, and best practices)

- *www.marketingsource.com* (Marketing articles for small businesses)

- *www.meetup.com* (Connects you to real-world meetings on any topic)

- *www.press-release-writing.com* (How to write press releases)

- *www.prweb.com* (Post and distribute your press release)

- *www.publicity.com* (Publicity articles and tips)

- *www.rushimprint.com* (Promotional items with quick turnaround time)

- *www.SEMList.com* (Search-engine marketing service buyer's guide)

- *www.wdfm.com* (Web digest for marketers)

CAREER MASTERS E-BRIDGE

Issue 362 – May 14, 2007

April's Newsletter

April's newsletter—***Career Masters Connection***—is now available on our website. In this month's issue, you'll find:

- *Extreme Resilience . . . Four Strategies for Success!* (by Beth Kennedy)
- *Member Spotlight on Jean Cummings* (by Beverly Harvey)
- *Recruiting and Employment Trends . . . Hope for the Future* (by Louise Kursmark)
- *Master Team Spotlight: Wendy Enelow's Journey to the Winner's Circle* (by Susan Whitcomb)

And, as always, I'll reprint one article at the end of each weekly E-Bridge. Enjoy!

April's Teleseminars

We are offering our members two great teleseminars this month:

- **Friday, April 13** – *Resume Strategies for Challenging Client Circumstances* (presenter – Deb Dib)
- **Friday, April 27** – *The Author Advantage: Insider Secrets To Getting A Book Published* (presenter – Louise Kursmark)

For complete class descriptions and registration, go to: http://www.cminstitute. com/teleseminars.html

Great Job Opportunity

Position: Career Development Center Director for Union College in Schenectady, NY (www.union.edu)

Founded in 1795, Union College, an independent liberal arts college, has distinguished itself through its unwavering commitment to excellence within and beyond the classroom. Reporting to the Vice President for Student Affairs, the Director is responsible for leading a high-quality staff dedicated to providing Union students and alumni with strong guidance as it relates to career planning/development initiatives. Responsibilities include providing long-range vision for the office, offering supervision and professional development for staff, and building collaborations with the College Relations division.

This position requires a high-energy, creative manager and leader who has a demonstrated record of success, preferably in the field of Career Services or related disciplines. A master's degree in higher education administration or a related discipline is preferred. Eight to ten years of progressively responsible experience in Career Services or a related field are required. Non-traditional backgrounds with significant career-related management and administration experience will be seriously considered.

To apply: Include your resume and list of references and submit to the executive search firm assisting Union College: Thomas F. Molloy, President, Molloy Partners, 340 Broadway, Saratoga Springs, NY 12866, Fax: (518) 581-2832, Email: tom@molloypartners.com

Member Kudos

Kudos to **Louise Kursmark** of Best Impression Career Services in Reading, MA. Louise was a keynote speaker for the 24th Annual Partners in Business Human Resources Seminar at Utah State University last week. In addition, her website, www.yourbestimpression.com, recently redesigned by Acorn Creative, was named "Best Corporate Site" at the recent New Hampshire Internet Awards. Double congratulations to you, Louise!

Congratulations to **Daisy Wright**, CDP BA CTM of The Wright Career Solution in Brampton, Canada. Daisy has just published her first book, *No Canadian Experience, Eh?*, a first-of-its-kind handbook that focuses primarily on the job-search process for new immigrants to Canada. As a result of her book, she's been interviewed by two local newspapers including a great article in *The Brampton Guardian*: http://www.thebramptonguardian.com/brampton/lifestyle/article/19902. We're delighted to see things going so very well for you, Daisy!

Stats, Sites & Stuff

Manpower Employment Outlook Survey (released March 2007)

These are the net-employment outlooks on a seasonally adjusted basis for each of the 10 industries:

- Mining, 26%, down from 29% who planned to hire in the first quarter
- Wholesale and retail trade, 20%, down from 22%
- Services, 19%, down from 23%

- Transportation and public utilities, 19%, up from 17%
- Non-durables manufacturers, 18%, flat from 18%
- Durable-goods manufacturers, 17%, down from 18%
- Finance, insurance and real estate, 17%, up from 15%
- Construction, 16%, down from 18%
- Public administration, 16%, down from 18%
- Education, 15%, down from 17%

Sources: Market Watch.com article, http://digbig.com/4rxgs
Related Report from BLS: "Employment Situation Summary," http://www.bls.gov/news.release/empsit.nr0.htm

Workforce.com Adds Blogs, Podcasts

They've added new features to the site, and expect to bring you more in the next few months. Check out their blogs, including staff writer Ed Frauenheim's "China Matters" reports. His blog joins "The Business of Management." Workforce.com is also introducing podcasts to the site, and as part of their special global report, they're kicking off with interviews of workforce management leaders in China. Visit: http://www.workforce.com/section/01/ (Source: Workforce Week, March 11-16 Newsletter)

For 50+ Job Seekers: RetirementJobs.com is a site for both job seekers and employers. Additionally, Robert Half International (RHI) and RetirementJobs.com have formed a strategic partnership in which RHI will provide job listings and career management content on RetirementJobs.com. Visit: http://retirementjobs.com.

This Week's Featured Article

EXTREME RESILIENCE:
Four Strategies for Career Success!

Beth B. Kennedy, MS, CAGS, CLTMC
Benatti Training & Career Development
BBK771@yahoo.com

Stress . . . we all have it! Good or bad, sometimes motivating and sometimes debilitating. This year has been a stressful one for me. After 15 years of providing career coaching to a large company, I was asked by the new manager to discontinue my services. In a state of shock and disbelief I questioned, *"Why? Was it my competence . . . my value . . . my impact . . . my style?"* I asked if I could provide the proper transition to these employees who were dealing with the stress of this major merger. To my surprise, I was retained for another three months to provide the necessary coaching to assist these individuals on their path. I wondered why, as painful as this was, I was doing okay most days. I was told by a close friend, *"You are handling this so well because you are so resilient."* The Merriam-Webster dictionary defines resilience as *an ability to recover from or adjust to misfortune or change.*

As a result of this major merger, I provided career coaching to many employees whose jobs had been eliminated, to some who had decided to take the offered package, and to others who had decided that it was the right time to take a different career path. As I traveled the journey with them, providing them support through the career development process, I realized the debilitating effect of stress. I noticed that individuals with extreme resilience were able to navigate much more effectively through the process. I found four common strategies that these resilient individuals had as part of their toolbox:

1. Stress management was a habit.
2. They had positive supportive people in their life.
3. They focused on weekly goal setting.
4. They had the confidence to move forward.

One of my clients, an attorney with the company, was so proactive at every coaching session. Although frustrated by the interview process, she had the most positive attitude. At my stress management check-in, she shared with me that stress management was an integral part of her action plan. She exercised regularly! Every week she accomplished her job search goals but never stopped focusing on her exercise program. Now at the next stage, she is getting job interviews and is moving forward with her vision. It is so easy when one is out of a job or under stress to stop focusing on self-care. This is definitely when we need it most. This is **Strategy 1:** *We need to focus on self-care regularly so that we can move smoothly through our personal and professional journey successfully.*

Another of my clients was told that he would need to go abroad for a few weeks for his company—in the middle of an MBA program and with a highly demanding job. I wondered how he would manage this. I provided many coaching sessions on the phone to Poland as his one-week stay turned into two and he ended up being away most of the summer. How did he manage this stress? **Strategy 2:** *Surround yourself with positive supportive people!* His wife understood how passionate he was in seeing this project end successfully, his graduate professors were flexible and understood the situation, he connected with colleagues in Poland who made work fun, and he found that having a coach gave him the opportunity to set goals as part of his regular routine. This individual's extreme resilience is definitely moving him forward in his career.

Another client, who had been asked to be on the transition team for the next six months, is wondering why she said yes. It is so stressful seeing her colleagues leave and working on projects that may or may not have a major impact. When we explore what keeps her going, it is her *focus on goal setting* (**Strategy 3**). She is someone who already has a regular exercise program and supportive friends, and although going to work right now is stressful, she finds that setting her weekly goals keeps her motivated and moving forward. Every week she focuses on one small step that will get her closer to the day when she will open her own consulting business. I know that part of the reason she was asked to remain temporarily with the company was not just her savvy competence but her extreme resilience.

During the three months of transitioning with my coaching clients, I noticed that my emotions were like a roller coaster. I felt my confidence lacking and my usual high energy level dwindling. I realized that with the stress of this change, I was not practicing my own usual stress management strategies. I realized that I needed to become proactive and focus on my coaching model for success. I started with step one and again began attending my weekly yoga class and returned to my regular exercise routine. When I reached out to my close friends who energize me, I felt so reconnected. I then realized I was in a state of shock, omitting my weekly goal setting. I took control! It felt so great to now wake up on Monday and write down goals for my business, personal life, etc. The best surprise was that I felt so reenergized and could feel my confidence and passion as a coach renewed. I could not believe how effective these four steps were! Within one month I received a brand new major training client and 10 new coaching clients!

As I mentioned, stress can be debilitating but also energizing. At the end of the three months, while informing another high-level individual at this company of my transition, she proposed that my services be utilized in a different manner. My career-coaching role was important in the past, but there was now a need for someone to focus on leadership and executive coaching. To my fortunate timing, I had completed my leadership coaching certification this year as part of my own personal goal setting. I thought it might be a great partnership with my career coaching. I have learned a lot from this experience and believe that my extreme resilience is the reason why I have continued to move forward as a coach, seeing my own business develop in ways I had always dreamed.

Today, think about your resilience. Choose one new goal for this month so that you are better prepared to cope with the stress of life. Whether looking for a new job or striving to be more successful at work or in your personal life, focusing on your extreme resilience will make the difference! Remember the four steps:

1. Make stress management a habit.
2. Seek positive support.
3. Focus on weekly goal setting.
4. Believe in yourself!

Wendy

Wendy S. Enelow, CCM, MRW, JCTC, CPRW
Executive Director – Career Masters Institute
2265 Walker Road, Coleman Falls, VA 24536
Phone: 434-299-5600
Fax: 434-299-7150
Email: wendy@cminstitute.com
Website: www.cminstitute.com

Career Masters Institute: Your Bridge to SUCCESS!

INFORM | INNOVATE | INSPIRE

5 Customers, Clients, and Patrons:
Can't Live With Them; Can't Live Without Them!

L ET'S FACE IT. YOUR BUSINESS is nothing without customers. If no one buys your products, it simply doesn't matter how good they are, how well they perform, or how unique they are. If no one uses your services, it doesn't matter that they're remarkably more effective, unique, or impactful than other similar services. Without customers, nothing about your business really matters because there won't be any business.

Building a new venture requires that you devote a tremendous amount of time to many different things—business planning and development, financing, sales, marketing, pricing, operations design, accounting, staffing, and much more. However, few things matter as much as your ability to build your customer base and then, even more importantly, retain those customers as your business continues to grow, expand, and become more profitable. An uncompromising commitment to consistently high-quality customer service is the cornerstone of every successful business venture!

It is important to note that, depending on the type of business you own, you will either have customers, clients, or patrons. These terms are used interchangeably throughout this chapter and this entire book. To help you better clarify which word is most appropriate for your business, consider the following:

- **Customers:** Manufacturing, Transportation, Retail, Sales
- **Clients:** Health Care, Law, Consulting, Insurance, Professional Services
- **Patrons:** Food Service/Restaurants, Hospitality

This chapter is divided into two primary sections. The first section highlights the 10 success factors for customer relationship management (CRM):

1. Build a Customer-Centric Organization
2. Make the Process Easy
3. *Touch* Your Customers
4. Embrace Your Customers
5. Speak Your Customers' Language
6. Be Friendly and Personable
7. Create a Professional Voice-Mail Message
8. Make It Easy to Return Your Call
9. Let Your Customers Know They're Valued
10. Own Your Customer Relationships

The degree to which this information will be relevant to you depends entirely on the type of business you're launching. If you'll be dealing directly with clients, either in person, on the phone, or through an exclusive online service, then CRM is a vital link to your success. These types of businesses rely heavily on an entrepreneur's ability to build and sustain long-term client relationships, and then leverage those relationships to get client

If you are dealing directly with clients, CRM is vital to your success.

referrals. It's all about the connection you're able to establish and the quality of service that you provide when you own and operate a customer-centric or service-centric business venture (as you read about in Chapters 2 and 3).

If you're starting an Internet-based product sales business where your entire goal is to build volume, then your focus on CRM is important, but to a somewhat lesser degree. In this situation, your focus will be on penetrating new markets, building new sales channels, expanding advertising reach, and more, to aggressively build your volume and capture market share. These types of businesses generally do not have the same level of direct client contact as businesses that are more focused on the individual client relationship. Rather, these businesses are often referred to as economic-centric where volume is the #1 driver of the business model (as explained in Chapters 2 and 3).

The second section of this chapter focuses in detail on the three essential steps to building, managing, and maintaining your customer base. All three of these components are critical functions for each and every successful entrepreneurial venture, and must be a key focus in your business:

1. Customer Profiling and Targeting

2. Customer Service Delivery

3. Customer Satisfaction and Retention

Key Success Factors for Customer Relationship Management

There are certain critical concepts and behaviors that you must understand in order to build a strong, profitable, and sustainable customer base. These concepts are vital to the long-term growth and success of your entrepreneurial venture (particularly if you're in a client-focused business, service, or industry), and must become an immediate and core component of each and every function within your organization.

Build a Customer-Centric Organization

Companies, which focus heavily on building and maintaining long-term client relationships, are commonly referred to as customer-centric or service-centric organizations. What this means is that everything about the company focuses on the client and the client relationship.

- Sales and marketing are focused on establishing and sustaining relationships with individual clients or client companies.

- Billing and accounting are focused on their responsiveness to customer calls, questions, and concerns.

- Manufacturing and operations are focused on producing and delivering the highest quality of products to ensure customer satisfaction.

- Information technology and telecommunications are focused on effectively supporting all customer-service and support functions.

- Human resources is focused on hiring individuals who understand the customer-centric business model.

If your goal is to build a company where customers are the cornerstone, then each and every function within your organization must be focused on the customer and the customer relationship. You must constantly strive to enhance each and every customer exchange by introducing new and improved CRM strategies and processes as your business grows. What's more, you can never lose sight of your goal to achieve close to 100% customer satisfaction and retention. You'll never achieve 100%; it's virtually impossible, for there will always be that one client who, no matter what you do, can never be satisfied. Be realistic in your expectations for yourself and your business!

Make the Process Easy

There is little more that you can do to propel your business to success than to make it easy for your customers to do business with you. If there are too many obstacles standing in the way—inefficiency, inaccessibility, poor customer response, unreturned phone calls, unmet delivery dates, incorrect billings, unfulfilled guarantees, and more—your customers will find somewhere else to do business. And, once you've lost a customer, it is extremely difficult to recapture them no matter what you do.

Make it easy for your customers to do business with you!

How many times have you found yourself in a situation where trying to buy a product or service was simply too difficult? I recently visited a major department store to buy a refrigerator. Easy enough, you'd think. However, it was anything but. I couldn't find a salesperson to assist me and, after 30 minutes when someone was finally available, they were unable to answer any of my questions. They did not know their products, they did not know their delivery schedule, and they did not know their warranty agreement. After an hour, I left in frustration and bought my new refrigerator elsewhere … at a store where I was waited on promptly, where the salesperson "knew" his products, and where the purchase was easy. Now, what do you think the chances are that I'll ever return to the first store I visited?

When I look back on my 25+ years as an entrepreneur, the one comment that I consistently received from my clients is that it was "easy to do business" with me. At first, that didn't seem like such a big deal and I would ask myself, "Shouldn't it always be easy to do business with a business?" But as the years passed and I personally had many less-than-positive dealings with other businesses (like trying to buy a refrigerator), I began to understand how truly important the concept of making the process easy was to my customers. I realized that if I were able to make it easier for my customers to do business with me than with my competitors, I would have a significant advantage within the market. And I have worked tirelessly to maintain that advantage throughout all of these years.

How can you make it easy for your customers to do business with you? Here are a few of the most critical factors impacting your ability to create an easy and seamless process for your customers:

- **Knock down any barriers** that stand between you and the customer, and make it easy to communicate with you via phone, email, or in person.

- **Make it easy to get information** from you, such as product literature, product samples, proposals, references, sales agreements, product/technology demonstrations, and more.

- **Deliver what you promise**, with no exceptions.

- **Meet all of your deadlines**, always and forever, barring any unforeseen emergencies.

- **Streamline the actual process** for buying your products, services, solutions, or other offerings.

- **Train your employees** on the strategies, techniques, and processes that will strengthen their customer relationships and their ability to provide efficient customer service and response.

- **Respond to your customers' inquiries** and concerns as quickly as possible. Note that it's often the customer who has to wait and wait to resolve a problem, get a question answered, or find additional information that is the most unhappy customer and has *not* found your process easy, efficient, or responsive.

Touch Your Customers

Twenty years ago, the vast majority of business was conducted face-to-face. You got to know whom you were doing business with, what they looked like, how they dressed, how firm their handshake was, and more. You looked them in the eye and got to know them.

Today's business world is a vastly different place than a generation ago. With the emergence of the Internet and associated e-commerce technologies, it is now possible—and quite likely—that a great deal of the business you do is with individuals whom you will never meet and companies that you may never have heard of before.

In a world where "remote" and "virtual" are now commonplace words in our business vocabulary, it is critical that you create systems and processes that will allow you to *touch* and *feel* your customers and allow your customers to *touch* and *feel* you and your business. Your goal is to create the perception that you are "right there with them," as they make a purchase, sign a contract for services, or evaluate the quality of your merchandise.

Obviously, if you own a retail business, the concept of direct customer interaction is not an issue. Hopefully, each and every day, customers will flock to your store, and you'll have the opportunity to communicate with them on a regular basis. Or, if you happen to be launching a machining company to service industrial designers and manufacturers in your local region, you'll most likely be meeting with your customers either at your facility or theirs.

However, if you're an Internet-based venture, the concepts of *touch* and *feel* become extremely important, whether you're offering products, selling services, or delivering telecommunications solutions. This is when you'll need to focus your energies on creating processes that will allow your customers to get to know you and your company. Otherwise, you'll simply be one of millions of cyberspace companies who are "out there," yet customers never really *feel* your presence.

For some companies—those offering a one-shot sale—this can be okay. For example, if you're selling discontinued Valentine's Day gift items through your website, most of your customers will only shop once. If you have the product they want, they'll buy, and the customer interaction is over.

However, if you're like most other companies, who want to capture and retain their customer base, you'll need to design and implement strategies that will allow you to reach out beyond cyberspace and become a "real person" or "real company" to your customers. To help you accomplish that, I've outlined some of my favorite strategies and actions that you can begin developing and implementing today as you build your new entrepreneurial venture.

- **Capture information** about each and every one of the unique visitors to your website, whenever possible. This might include their names, email addresses, mailing addresses, and/or phone numbers. This is remarkably valuable information and will allow you to build a list of well-qualified prospects. However, be forewarned, that it is often difficult to capture such information since many, many people will not want to provide their name and contact information. One great strategy to capture this information is to offer something for free—a free newsletter or article, a free product sample, a coupon, or anything else you can offer that entice individuals to provide their names and contact information, and which is either no-cost or very low-cost to you.

- **Mail business cards** and brochures. Whenever possible, mail business cards and brochures to your prospective clients. When they receive this in the mail, all of a sudden you're no longer a cyberspace entity. Rather, they can "touch and feel" your materials which creates a much stronger perception of who you are, what your business offers, and the quality of your services. Instantly, you and your business come alive. Do not ever believe for one moment that your website replaces the traditional print brochure . . . it does not. For more information on writing, designing, and producing high-impact print brochures, refer back to that section in Chapter 4.

- **Prominently and attractively display your products** on your website. Have you ever visited a website where the products were difficult to view either because of a poor-quality photograph or images that were too small to see? Hire a professional photographer to take high-resolution pictures of your merchandise for your website and/or a professional web designer who knows the intricacies of website design and marketing.

- **Include your biography**, along with the biographies of your key employees, on your website. You may also want to include a picture of yourself and your team so your customers can see whom they're doing business with.

Embrace Your Customers

The key to success in virtually any business is your ability to build strong and enduring customer relationships. To achieve that, you must understand the concept of embracing each and every one of your customers by making them feel special, valuing their business, responding to their needs, and being accessible.

People want to do business with people whom they like and who like them. It's that simple. As such, if you are able to communicate—through your words, actions, behaviors, and follow-through—that you indeed do value each customer's business, you will have reached a remarkable summit in your business. Those clients will continue to do business with you, with little or no regard for your competition, as long as you continue to create such an atmosphere of customer care.

What's more, your clients will work for you! They'll refer you to their friends, colleagues, business associates, and others, providing you with the opportunity to build your customer base with no additional effort. Your satisfied customers will be your sales team, promoting you, your business, your services, and your products without you even knowing it. Before long, your phone will ring, your email box will fill up, and prospective customers will be "knocking at your door."

What's more, these referrals are already pre-sold on the quality of your products and services, since an impartial third-party source has referred them. Of course, that does not mean that each referral will be a definite sale, but it certainly puts you well ahead of the game when compared to customers whom you are selling "cold."

As a business owner, you will enjoy tremendous power and success if you are able to create the perception that you are embracing each and every client, and then leveraging those relationships to build even more relationships and further build your sales volume.

Speak Your Customers' Language

There is nothing better than doing business with someone who understands your business! And the very best way to demonstrate that you understand your customers' business is to speak their language, use their lingo, and know their jargon. Obviously, this concept is most critical when you're involved in business-to-business (B2B) sales.

Often we hear the term "keywords" in reference to resume writing and job search. However, keywords are a critical component of every sales process, whether selling yourself for a new job or selling an industrial-ventilation system to General Motors. The point of keywords is to:

- **Communicate a "big" message with just one or two "little" words.** For example, the keyword phrase, *supply-chain management*, communicates knowledge of logistics, vendor sourcing, inventory planning, materials management, warehousing, distribution, and more.

- **Position yourself as a part of, or knowledgeable about, a specific industry or profession.** For example, by using the phrase "uploading PDF files," you immediately communicate to a customer that you are skilled in the latest technology of the printing business and, therefore, will probably save them money.

The latter point is what is most critical to your success as an entrepreneur. By positioning yourself as part of a particular customer's industry or profession, you will give yourself a measurable advantage over your competition. As such, if your customers come principally from just a few key industries or professions, start learning the language. You can read articles, skim books, search keywords on the Internet, and more. In fact, much of what you'll learn will come directly from your customer interactions!

Connect with your clients by communicating that you know who they are and, therefore it's implied, what they need. You'll find that it will make an immediate and significant difference in your ability to close new sales and retain your targeted customer base.

Be Friendly and Personable

Be likable! All too often business people are so concerned about being extremely professional that they forget how important it is to be friendly and personable. These concepts are not mutually exclusive! Rather, you can be professional in your business relationships and your demeanor, while still presenting yourself as engaging and likable. The reality is that people want to do business with people they like, and there is no better way to build those customer bonds than to be friendly and take the time necessary to communicate with, and be responsive to, your customers.

Consider truly successful people you know and you'll realize a common characteristic that almost all of them share—they are open and friendly. It's as though they're silently communicating, *"Come up and talk to me. I'm all yours!"* In turn, others are attracted to them (the Law of Attraction) and want to do business with them.

To accelerate your success and the success of your business, be sure that you exude that same kind of genuine openness and approachability.

Create a Professional Voice-Mail Message

Like it or not, voice mail has become the status quo. Consider the number of times in the past month that you've called someone, only to get their voice mail when they're out of the office, with a customer, on the phone, or otherwise engaged. Inevitably, the same thing is going to happen when people call you and you're simply unavailable to receive their call.

Most people think that the primary function of a voice-mail message is to notify a caller that you're "out of the office." Wrong! A truly effective voice-mail message is really a marketing communication that allows you to sell your products and service, highlight the benefits of doing business with your company, and otherwise merchandise what you want to sell to prospective clients. Here's a great example:

> *"Hi! You've reached the office of Wendy Enelow, one of the leading career consultants in the country and author of more than 25 books on job search and career management. I work exclusively with top executives worldwide to help them strategize and execute winning search campaigns, and would be delighted to chat with you about your particular situation. I'm not available to take your call right now, but please leave your name and number, and I'll get right back in touch. If you'd like to learn more about my credentials and services, and how they will benefit you, please visit www.wendyenelow.com. Thanks and have a great day!"*

Note the brevity of the above message. It is imperative that you keep your voice-mail messages as brief as possible. How many times have you placed a call and then had to listen to a message that's 45, 60, 90, or more seconds long? It's as though it will never end. Don't make your clients wait too long or chances are likely that they will hang up and you will have lost the sale. Remember, in addition to customer calls, you will be getting many calls from colleagues, associates, vendors, employees, and others who simply want to leave a message, without having to repeatedly listen to your lengthy message over and over.

Make It Easy to Return Your Call

How many times have you had to listen to a phone message two or three times to get the caller's phone number? It happens to me all of the time and is unbelievably frustrating, particularly when the phone message is lengthy and the number is very quickly squeezed in at the end. To ensure that you don't do that to others, repeat your phone number twice—slowly and clearly —whenever leaving a phone message. Leave it at the beginning of your message and then repeat it again near the end of your message.

In addition, don't leave more than two numbers where people can reach you. When you leave three, four, or more numbers, it becomes too much of a chore to track you down. Take advantage of the latest telecommunications technology that allows you to link all of your phone numbers and make it easy for someone to return your call!

Let Your Customers Know They're Valued

Clients love to be appreciated and there is little in business that can mean more than a handwritten thank-you note (not an email message!), a holiday greeting card, or small gift. The fact that you've taken the time to write a note, mail a card, or purchase a gift instantly communicates to your customer the fact that you value your relationship with them and appreciate their business. What's more, these things are easy and inexpensive.

Consider the following situations when it's most important to acknowledge your clients:

- **Send a note to thank your clients for their business or to thank them for referring others to your business.** I have one client who has referred more than 75 other clients to me, and I'm sure to send a thank-you note each and every time. My client tells me that he saves every card I send and is now working on his second shoebox full! Just think about how much he values our business relationship, the quality of service I provide, and, most importantly, the value I place on his relationship with me and my company!

- **Send holiday-greeting cards to all of your customers.** When you read Chapter 8, *Technology: It's a Tool, Not a Solution*, you'll learn the many reasons why it's so important to keep an accurate database of all of your customers. For the purposes of this discussion about customer-relationship management, you can easily generate a set of mailing labels from your database, allowing you to quickly prepare and distribute holiday cards to everyone. Be sure to handwrite your name—at a minimum—since pre-printed cards do not communicate the same "personal" connection. Again, this small task communicates a huge message to your clients and will help you to continue differentiating yourself from your competitors.

- **Send small gifts to your customers who spend "big bucks" with you.** Each year, you'll find that there is a select group of customers with whom you've worked very closely or who have spent a great deal of money with you and your company. For these individuals, I recommend a small business gift as an acknowledgment of their patronage and their continued relationship with your company. Gifts you might consider include leather portfolios, desk calendars (ones that will be used and not simply tossed into a desk drawer), journals, fruit baskets, chocolates, wine (when appropriate), gift certificates, or something that coincides directly with your business. For example, if you're a professional photographer, you might send a print of one of your favorite photos. Gifts do not have to be expensive. The thought alone is what delivers the most value to your customers.

Own Your Customer Relationships

The most important concept in customer-relationship management is what is referred to as "owning the customer relationship." What does that mean? Simply put, it means that your customers are your customers as long as you continue to provide them with high-quality, valuable products and services. In essence, they're yours to keep as long as you, your employees, and your business don't do anything to drive them away.

Consider the following . . . whether deliberate or not, you've been able to build rapport, establish trust, and deliver on your promises to each of your customers. As such, you've captured those customer relationships and now own them forever. The potential exists, if you remain in business, that you can service each of those clients for five, 10, 15, 20, or even more years. You are in control of those relationships and can retain them for as long as you want, barring any unforeseen changes in your business operations, the economic climate, the marketplace, and/or a number of other variables that may not be under your control.

Think back and try to remember how you accomplished that. Specifically, what did you do to build so many successful client relationships? Why do your clients value you, your employees, and your business? Why do your clients trust you and the products and/or services that you offer? How have you managed to build so many relationships with so many different clients? How have you managed to accomplish so much?

If you can answer those questions, you will have found the key that is essential to building, retaining, and favorably managing your customer relationships for years and years to come. If you can do that, you will succeed!

Three Essential Steps to Building, Managing, and Maintaining Your Customer Base

The following step-by-step process for customer development and management lies at the foundation of every successful business venture, whether it's the local dry cleaners on Main Street in Albuquerque, the plastics manufacturing company in St. Louis, or Bill Gates's billion-dollar Microsoft enterprise.

Before any of these companies opened their doors, they had to do their research and be able to decisively answer the following questions:

- Who are my customers?
- How can I capture them?
- What are the best ways to deliver my products or services to them?
- What can I do to ensure their satisfaction?
- How can I keep them as customers?

What's more, once a company is up and running, these same questions need to be addressed on a regular basis as the company grows, changes, and moves forward. Nothing is stagnant, including your customer base. The more successful your business becomes, the more it may change, diversify, specialize, or re-invent itself over and over and over. Hand-in-hand with that evolution in your business will be a change in your customer base.

To help you prepare yourself to answer those questions, I've focused this section on the three key steps to building, managing, and maintaining your customer base:

- **Customer Profiling and Targeting** (identifying and capturing your customers)

- **Customer Service** (servicing your customers)

- **Customer Satisfaction and Retention** (satisfying and keeping your customers)

Step 1: Customer Profiling and Targeting

I'll assume that you've completed step one in your business planning process and identified the particular type of company that you want to launch. As you read earlier in this book, I strongly recommend that you select a venture that closely matches your core skills, qualifications, interests, and expertise. For example, if you're a network engineer, it's much easier to launch a tele-communications company than it is to own and operate a restaurant. That is, of course, unless you're a chef on the side!

What's more, if you focus your business in industries and professions that you know well, you should already have some knowledge of who your primary customers will be. If you're reaching into an entirely new market, you'll have to do more extensive research to be sure that you're focusing your sales, marketing, and business-development efforts (and money!) on the *right* customer market.

The next logical question, then, is precisely how do you profile potential customers? Taking it one step further, how do you identify them, let them know about you, communicate with them, and entice them to do business with you?

The answer to that question is straightforward. You start at the very beginning and then work your way through a four-step process to profile and target your core customer base. These four steps are:

1. Researching
2. Identifying
3. Messaging
4. Capturing

1. Researching

Step one in identifying your customer base is to launch an extensive market-research effort. Your objective is to collect as much information as possible about the customers that buy the same (or similar) types of products and services that you will be offering.

- Will you be selling to individuals, other businesses, or a combination of both?

- Are your customers restricted to a certain geography or are they nationwide or worldwide?

- Do your customers represent a certain demographic (e.g., age group, socioeconomic status, race, ethnicity, educational level)?

- Do your customers have a common need (e.g., HVAC repair parts, technology training, healthcare services)?

- Do your customers share a common interest or similar lifestyle (e.g., NASCAR, animal husbandry, yoga, theater)?

To find this information and more, we recommend the following sources:

- **Internet Searches.** The Internet has opened a whole new world and provides us with access to information that was never before so easy to assemble. For example, if your goal is to start a retail clothing store in your city and you want to learn about the socioeconomic status of individuals living in different neighborhoods, go to *www.google.com* and type in the words "Cincinnati + demographics" and a long list of websites will pop up that provide precisely that information. It couldn't be any easier!

- **Networking.** Think about all of the people that you know—people whom you know professionally, personally, socially, and casually. Chances are that it's a relatively long list. Then, think about what these people know and whom they know, and you'll realize that they're an excellent source of information on a whole host of topics. For example, if your goal is to start an industrial-production company that will supply parts to refrigeration manufacturers nationwide, go to *www.google. com* and type in the words "refrigeration manufacturers" and you'll find pages and pages of companies in that particular industry. You can then visit each of their websites to learn more about the specific equipment they manufacture and whether or not your parts are what they need. If not, it's time to rethink your parts and your business plan.

- **Professional Associations.** Professional associations are a wonderful channel for learning about specific industries and professions, and accessing *insider* information that may not be publicly available. No matter the type of venture that you're considering, there will most likely be at least one, if not several, professional associations that can provide valuable information. For example, if you're starting a technology-consulting company and you want to identify firms in your region that need those specific technology services, join the Computer Security Institute and any other related associations so that you can begin to immerse yourself within the industry and identify your prime customer targets.

2. Identifying

Once you've completed the research stage, you should have accumulated a great deal of information (AKA market intelligence) about your prospective customers. The next step is to analyze all of that information so that you can pinpoint the precise customer markets that you want to target. Here's an example of how that works:

Let's say that you've decided to start a financial-consulting and investment firm. You've done your preliminary research and identified thousands of prospective customers within a 50-mile radius of your office. This includes all homes with an annual income of greater than $50,000 since they're the primary market that most financial consultants target. However, your firm is going to offer unique financial-planning services that will not be of interest to all of those potential investors. Instead, the individuals that you want to target are those who are under 55 years of age because they are more comfortable investing in higher-risk opportunities than individuals who are 55 years of age and older.

Now, what have you accomplished thus far in your customer profiling efforts? First, you did your research and identified the total potential customer base. You've then taken it one step further, defined additional characteristics of your customer base, and clearly identified those individuals who would be most interested in your products or services. Once this list or database is finalized, you will have completed the first two critical steps in customer profiling—research and identification—and can then proceed through the remaining two steps.

3. Messaging

Now that you've researched and identified your target customer base, your next challenge is to define the message that you want to communicate to them.

- Do you want to tell them why your products or services are better than the competition's?

- Do you want to highlight the benefits of using your products or services?

- Do you want to tell them that your products or services are less expensive?

- Do you want to tell them that your products or services are of the highest quality?

Once you've defined your message, the next phase in this step is to determine the best vehicle for communicating that message. In other words, how can you reach out and grab the attention of your prospective customers? Based on the extensive research that you did in steps one and two of customer profiling and targeting, you should have developed a good sense of the best strategies for communicating with your targeted audience. Are you going to:

- Write and design print advertisements for newspapers, magazines, and other publications?

- Write and design online advertisements for placement on various websites that would attract the specific clientele that you are targeting?

- Send email messages showcasing your products or services?

- Write and design coupon mailers for local or national distribution?

- Author articles about products, services, technologies, processes, or other information that will build your market visibility and credibility, encouraging customers to do business with you?

- Speak at professional meetings, conferences, and workshops to get yourself and your company in front of the *right* buying audience?

For more information on messaging, advertising and marketing communications, refer back to Chapter 4 where these topics were discussed in much greater detail.

4. Capturing

Capturing new customers is more commonly referred to as sales, the actual process of selling your products or services to an individual or a business customer. Whether your sales are done in person, on the phone, or via the Internet, your ability to capture new customers and entice them to do business with you is one of the most vital functions you'll perform in your role as entrepreneur.

Hopefully, you closely read Chapter 4, which focuses on sales and marketing in great detail. If not, now is the time to refer back to that chapter and learn what it takes to capture customers and win in today's intensely competitive marketplace.

Step 2: Customer Service

No matter your specific entrepreneurial venture, delivering products and services to your customers is, most likely, your primary objective. And, in fact, it doesn't really matter how effective you are in customer profiling, targeting, and capturing if you can't deliver what you've promised. The delivery process is at the root of the entire customer-management function and, therefore, must be firmly established within your company.

There are certain standards by which successful companies operate in order to ensure that they deliver consistently superior service to their customers. These "rules of the road" include:

- **Always deliver on time.** There are virtually no excuses for not delivering products or services on time, barring any emergencies or catastrophes. If you've promised that a customer's package will be shipped on Thursday, then be sure that you ship on Thursday. If you've promised to finish a technology-consulting engagement within three weeks, then be sure that you're done! Customers expect you to deliver what you promise, when you promise it. If you're perpetually late in your delivery, word will spread and it won't matter how good your product or service is. The bad publicity associated with continually late orders can have a negative impact on your company for a long time to come.

- **Exceed your customers' expectations for quality.** No matter what industry or profession you are in, your ability to consistently provide quality products and services to your customers is essential. No one wants to purchase anything that is second-rate! If you truly want to excel within your entrepreneurial venture, then you must be certain that you're delivering the very best. Your commitment to quality must transcend your entire organization, from the manufacturing floor to the warehouse to each customer's door. If customers can't get quality from you, they'll shop elsewhere!

- **Always be on time!** If you have a client appointment scheduled for Friday at 11 am, be there and be ready. Again, there are no excuses. How many times have you sat in an office waiting for a doctor, an attorney, or an accountant? Your appointment time came and went. You continued to wait. With each passing moment, you became more and more annoyed. Is that how you want your clients to feel? Demonstrate that you value your clients and their time by scheduling your time wisely!

- **Conduct customer surveys and focus groups.** There is no better way to collect information about the customer experience at your company than to ask your customers! With relative ease, you can create a survey that should provide you with critical information about how each customer perceived their experience with your company, what they would change, what they would improve, what they would eliminate, and more. What's more, there are now online survey tools that are easy, efficient, and reasonably priced (*www.surveymonkey.com*). Spend the time that is necessarily to collect and analyze this data, identify trends, and then use it to improve your service-delivery competencies.

Step 3: Customer Satisfaction and Retention

Bottom-line, the name of the game in any successful entrepreneurial venture is customer satisfaction. Happy customers will come back to buy more; happy customers will refer others to you and your company.

As I outlined in the previous section, delivering what you promise, when you promise, is essential to fulfilling your customers' needs and expectations, and ensuring their satisfaction. Once you're able to do this, most likely those customers will continue to be your customers for a long time to come. And, that's wonderful news on many different levels:

- **There is no cost to the sale.** Whenever you sell something to a new client, there is a cost associated with capturing that client. Typically, I'm referring to advertising, marketing, and/ or promotional costs. However, when you sell something to an existing client, there is no cost to the sale! You've already captured that customer and you're simply adding additional revenues. Retaining and re-selling to your existing customer base is a wonderful way to build your business without having to increase your advertising, marketing, and selling costs!

- **Your customers already know *how* to do business with you.** Once you've worked with a customer one time, they understand how your business works and what they can expect. They know what merchandise and services you offer, they know how to buy them, they know how to pay, they understand about delivery charges, and more. Then, when they return to do business with you a second time, third time, or 20th time, the actual process of doing business is more streamlined and efficient, making it an even better interaction between both you and your customer.

- **Your customers have realistic expectations about the quality of your product or service.** If they bought from you in the past and they're returning for a repeat sale, you can rest assured that your customers are satisfied with the quality that your company offers. As such, there are no surprises and this, in and of itself, can make for a much smoother and happier purchasing experience.

- **You and your company will save money.** Servicing repeat clients allows you to save money in several different ways. First and foremost, as mentioned previously, there are no marketing, selling, advertising, or promotional costs associated with capturing existing clients. Just as significant, your costs for servicing that client may also be reduced, since less manpower will be involved in collecting client information, processing repeat orders, and managing the administrative functions of customer service and relationship management.

With all of that in mind, your challenge is to design and implement business plans, processes, programs, and operations that are focused on retaining your customer base while you continue to build new client relationships and expand into new customer markets.

Here are some of my favorite strategies for long-term customer retention:

- **Stay in touch.** It is essential that you routinely communicate with your clients so that you and your business remain in their consciousness. Consider writing a monthly or quarterly newsletter, mailing or emailing information about new products and services, promoting special offers, or adding new product or industry information to your website. These efforts help to keep your company visible to your clients and encourage additional purchases and customer referrals.

- **Make it easy** for your clients to contact you. Have you ever had to search and search to find a phone number or email address for a company you did business with in the past? You enjoyed working with them, the quality of their products was excellent, and you're ready to purchase something else. However, they relocated over a year ago, their old phone number has been disconnected, and you can't find them on the Internet. If this happens to you, chances are they'll do business elsewhere. As a company owner, it is your responsibility to reach **out to each and every customer** to alert them to changes in location, phone, or email contact. If you drop the ball and move on without them, you will have lost one of the most valuable assets that you own—your existing customer base. Be sure that this doesn't happen to you!

- **The client is ALWAYS right—USUALLY.** How many times have you heard that? Probably more than you can count. However, it is true, no matter your profession—career coach, retail sales clerk, industrial designer, Internet-based publisher, or automotive mechanic. Your clients hire you to do a specific job for them or provide them with a specific product or service. You do your part and they pay. Sounds pretty easy, doesn't it?

And, usually, it is pretty easy. If you deliver what you promised in a timely manner and charge your customers what you agreed on, then there shouldn't be any problem. However, no matter how precisely you operate your business and how magnificently you manage your client relationships, there will always be a handful of customers who complain or are dissatisfied. There is simply no way around it.

In these instances, you want to work to satisfy that individual customer and retain that relationship. Therefore, in many instances, although you may believe that you're right, you want to respond in such a manner that your customer perceives that he or she is right. Consider this scenario:

> You own an Internet-based office-products company and one of your customers ordered a desk. When the shipment is received, the customer calls and is extremely unhappy with the quality of the product, although you know that it's made of fine teak wood. You have two options in this instance:
>
> 1. You can argue with the customer and try to convince him or her of the exceptional quality of the product, knowing that this is probably a losing battle.
>
> 2. You can simply process a return, refund the money, and, hopefully, impress your customer with the quality and responsiveness of your service.

Only you can determine the actual value of each customer relationship and how far you want to bend to satisfy each and every person. This will depend on the type of business that you're operating, the specific customer markets that you service, and the level of relationship that you have with each client. Let your customers be right, but do implement sound business practices to be sure that you're not taken advantage of.

If you follow the preceding advice:

- Your name and company will become synonymous with high-quality service and excellence.

- You can gradually increase your prices (and your profits) to keep pace with the demand.

- You can sell new services and new products to those clients who already know the value of what you offer. New services and products mean increased revenues which, hopefully, equal more profits for both you and your company.

Perhaps the greatest benefit of all will be the constant stream of referrals you will receive. Happy clients refer other clients, who then refer others. If you are diligent, determined, and consistent, your business and client base will grow without a fortune having to be invested in advertising, marketing, and promotions. Let your satisfied clients sell for you!

Unload Troublesome Clients

This entire chapter has focused on capturing, servicing, and maintaining your customer base. What happens, however, when you have a customer whom you no longer want to work with? It may be that they are consistently difficult to please, always have problems, never follow through on their end, are constantly complaining, are rude to you or your staff, are slow to pay their bills, or any one of a number of other issues that have negatively impacted your relationship with them. At some point, these types of clients will become too high-maintenance and you'll most likely want to rid yourself of them. Trust me . . . it happens in every business, every industry, and every market.

As the owner of your own entrepreneurial venture, you have tremendous power, including the power to say to a client, "I don't want to work with you any longer." Simply put, you can fire clients at your discretion. You certainly don't want this to be a common occurrence; however, at some point, the money is outweighed by the hassle and stress involved in selling to, and servicing, a particular client.

If you find yourself in this position, we strongly recommend that you handle the client situation with kid gloves because you never want to burn any bridges. When you're firing a client and telling them that you no longer want to work with them, try to do it as gently as possible and offer to give them other resources. Here's a great example:

> *"John, I think our working relationship has come to a close and hope that you will understand. I've certainly appreciated your business over the past few years, but I can see that we're starting to change directions and I'm concerned that I'm not meeting your needs. As such, I'd like to refer you to Gloria Jones at the ABC Manufacturing Company. I'm sure that she can handle all of your product needs. Can I give her your phone number?"*

The above is short and sweet, and does not open you up to lots of conversation about why you're "dismissing" the customer. Rather, you've clearly stated your position and offered a reasonable alternative. That is all you can be expected to do.

Recommended Resources for Customer Relationship Management

Books

- *180 Ways to Talk the Customer Service Talk* (Eric Harvey)
- *Award-Winning Customer Service: 101 Ways to Guarantee Great Performance* (Renee Evenson)
- *Be Our Guest: Perfecting the Art of Customer Service* (Disney Institute)
- *Best Practices in Customer Service* (Ron Zemk Woods)
- *Breakthrough Customer Service* (Stanley A. Brown)
- *Customer Service Made Easy* (Paul Levesque)
- *Customer Service Training 101* (Renee Evenson)
- *Delivering Knock Your Socks Off Service* (Perf Research Association)
- *E-Newsletters That Work: The Small Business Owner's Guide* (Michael J. Katz)
- *Great Customer Service on the Telephone* (Kristin Anderson)
- *Listen Up, Customer Service: A Guide to Develop Customer Loyalty* (David Cottrell and Mark C. Layton)
- *Magnetic Service: Secrets of Creating Passionately Devoted Customers* (Chip R. Bell and Bilijack R. Bell)
- *Monitoring, Measuring & Managing Customer Service* (Gary S. Goodman)
- *Multicultural Customer Service* (Leslie Aguilar and Linda Stokes)
- *Perfect Phrases for Customer Service* (Robert Bacal)
- *Super Service: Seven Keys to Delivering Great Customer Service … Even When You Don't Feel Like It! … Even When They Don't Deserve It!* (Jeff Gee and Val Gee)
- *Superior Customer Service: How to Keep Customers Coming Back to Your Business* (Dan W. Blacharski)
- *Total Customer Service: The Ultimate Weapon* (Davidow & Uttal)

- *Working Relationships* (Bob Wall)
- *The World of Customer Service* (Pattie Odgers)

Websites

- *www.bettermanagement.com* (CRM topics)
- *www.crma-northwest.org* (premier CRM informational forum for business professionals)
- *www.CRMwhitepapers.com* (free white papers)
- *www.gartner.com/2_events/conferences/crf8.jsp* (CRM summit information)
- *www.kdnuggets.com/websites/crm.html* (CRM news, events, case studies, and more)
- *www.pivotal.com* (free CRM white paper)
- *www.wdfm.com/publish/customer_relationship_management/index.htm* (CRM resource center)

6 Money:
Does It Grow on Your Tree?

UNLESS YOU HAPPEN TO BE a bookkeeper, accountant, financial consultant, or investment planner, chances are that managing your business finances will be one of the most challenging aspects of your entrepreneurial venture. The financial responsibilities of owning and operating a small business can be some of the most onerous and most difficult to manage. I'm best at making money—like most entrepreneurs—and not so great at preparing cash-flow statements!

This chapter is devoted to all of those monetary functions that will be an inherent part of your business venture—from operating and capital budgets, to cost and profit analysis, to quarterly and annual tax filings, to long-range financial planning. Although not what you'd consider the *fun* part of owning a business, these functions are critical to your initial financial viability and your long-term profitability.

This chapter begins with an **Entrepreneur's Dictionary of Essential Financial Terms** and then follows with information about all of the key financial components typical of most entrepreneurial ventures. You'll also find a number of formulas to help you calculate your dollars and percentages, along with several forms that will help you begin to build the financial structure of your business. Finally, the chapter ends with some strategic concepts that are critical to the financial success of virtually every entrepreneurial venture.

Remember, although this information may not be exciting, it is essential that you master these concepts so that you'll begin to understand your money—how it works, where it comes from, where it goes, what to do with it, and so much more.

The following financial terms are just a small sampling of the thousands of words related to bookkeeping, general accounting, cost accounting, finance, financial analysis, investment, and much more. For additional information on financial concepts that are particularly relevant to your business, consult these websites:

- *www.businessplansoftware.org/advice_glossary.asp*

- *www.finance-glossary.com/pages/home.htm*

- *www.nytimes.com/library/financial/glossary/bfglosm.htm*

- *www.ventureline.com/glossary.asp*

- *http://biz.yahoo.com/f/g/*

- *http://financial-dictionary.thefreedictionary.com/*

Entrepreneur's Dictionary of Essential Financial Terms

Accounting: The bookkeeping methods involved in making a financial record of business transactions and in the preparation of statements concerning the assets, liabilities, and operating results of a business.

Accounts Payable: Short-term debts incurred as a result of day-to-day business operations.

Accounts Receivable: Money due to your enterprise as a result of day-to-day operations.

Amortization: The repayment of a loan by installments.

Annual Report: Yearly record of a publicly held company's financial condition. It includes a description of the firm's operations, balance sheet, and income statement. SEC rules require that it be distributed to all shareholders. A more detailed version is called a 10-K.

Articles of Incorporation: Legal document establishing a corporation and its structure and purpose.

Asset: Real and intellectual property owned by a business that has positive financial value.

Balance Sheet: Also called a statement of financial condition, it is a summary of the assets, liabilities, and owners' equity in a company.

Break-Even Analysis: An analysis of the level of sales at which a project, product, service, and/or company would make zero profit.

Budget: A detailed schedule of financial activity, such as an advertising budget, a sales budget, a capital budget, or an operating budget.

Buyout: Purchase of a controlling interest (or percent of shares) of a company's stock. A leveraged buy-out (LBO) is done with borrowed money.

Capital: Financial investment required to initiate and/or operate a business.

Capital Budget: A firm's set of planned capital expenditures for the acquisition or improvement of long-term assets such as property, plant, or equipment.

Cash: Value of assets that can be converted into cash immediately, as reported by a company. Usually includes bank accounts and marketable securities.

Cash Flow: Transfer of monies into and out of a business.

Corporation: Legal entity that is separate and distinct from its owners. A corporation is allowed to own assets, incur liabilities, and sell securities, among other things.

Cost of Goods: Direct costs involved in producing a product or delivering a service, usually including labor and materials.

Cost of Sales: Cost of goods plus the expenses involved in selling and delivering the product or service.

Depreciation: Allocation of the purchase cost of an asset over its life.

Earnings: Net income of a company.

Earnings Before Interest and Taxes (EBIT): Financial measure defined as revenues less cost of goods sold, general, and administrative expenses. In other words, operating and non-operating profit before the deduction of interest and income taxes.

Equity: Represents ownership interest in a firm.

Finance: Discipline concerned with determining financial value and making financial decisions. The finance function allocates resources, which includes acquiring, investing, and managing resources.

Financial Plan: Financial blueprint for the financial future of a firm.

Fixed Asset: Long-lived property owned by a firm that is used by a firm in the production of its income. Tangible fixed assets include real estate, plant, and equipment. Intangible fixed assets include patents, trademarks, and customer recognition.

Gross Profit: Revenues less cost of sales.

Income Statement: Statement showing the revenues, expenses, and income (the difference between revenues and expenses) of a corporation over some period of time. Often referred to as a Profit and Loss Statement.

IRA/Keogh Accounts: Special accounts where you can save and invest, and the taxes are deferred until money is withdrawn.

Liability: Financial obligation, or the cash outlay that must be made at a specific time to satisfy the contractual terms of such an obligation.

Line of Credit: Informal arrangement between a bank and a customer, establishing a maximum loan balance that the bank will permit the borrower to maintain.

Liquid Asset: Asset that is easily and cheaply turned into cash—notably cash itself and short-term securities.

Net Income: Company's total earnings, reflecting revenues adjusted for costs of doing business, depreciation, interest, taxes, and other expenses.

Net Profit Margin: Net income divided by sales; the amount of each sales dollar left over after all expenses have been paid.

Net Worth: Assets minus liabilities.

Operating Budget: Budget for current expenses as distinct from financial transactions or permanent improvements.

Operating Cash Flow: Earnings before depreciation minus taxes. It measures the cash generated from operations, not counting capital spending or working capital requirements.

Partnership: Legal relationship between two or more individuals to conduct a specifically defined enterprise.

Pro-Forma Financial Statements: Financial statements as adjusted to reflect a projected or planned transaction.

Profit: Total revenues less total expenses.

Real Assets: Identifiable assets, such as buildings, equipment, patents, and trademarks.

Retained Earnings: Accounting earnings that are retained by the firm for reinvestment in its operations; earnings that are not paid out as dividends.

Revenue: Sales dollars produced by a company for the delivery of a product or service.

ROI (Return on Investment): Net profit divided by net worth; a financial ratio indicating the degree of profitability.

Shareholders' Equity: Company's total assets minus total liabilities. A company's net worth is the same thing.

Sole Proprietorship: Enterprise owned by a single individual.

Spreadsheet: Computer program that organizes numerical data into rows and columns on a computer screen; used for calculating and making adjustments based on new data.

Stock: Ownership of a corporation, which is represented by shares, which represent a piece of the corporation's assets and earnings.

Taxable Income: Gross income less established deductions.

Venture Capital: Investment in a start-up business that is perceived to have excellent growth prospects but does not have access to capital markets. Type of financing sought by early-stage companies seeking to grow rapidly.

Working Capital: Cash available to a business for its day-to-day operations.

Nuts and Bolts of Financial Management

Start-Up Financing

Launching a new business requires money, pure and simple. On the one hand, if you're starting a small, home-based business such as a fire-restoration service, your start-up capital may be relatively small (e.g., cleaning supplies and equipment, business cards, fliers for local businesses). On the other end of the spectrum, if you're purchasing an existing manufacturing company, your start-up requirements may be in the millions of dollars to pay for the company, the facility, the assets, the name, the goodwill, and much more.

Knowing that you will have start-up capital requirements, you need to immediately identify where you will get the money to not only fund your start-up, but also the initial operation of your business. No matter how strong your revenue projections, it always takes time for a new business to start generating a profit, and there is always a transition period following a change in ownership.

Most likely, your funding will come from one, or a combination, of these resources:

- Personal savings and/or investment accounts
- Bank loan
- Bank credit line
- Family loan
- Private investor
- Venture-capital group
- Business partner

To find information on capital-financing sources, visit the following websites:

Top 100 Venture Capital Firms
- *http://entrepreneur.com/vc100*

Top Micro-Friendly Business Banks
- *http://entrepreneur.com/bestbanks*

If you recall the discussion about business plans from Chapter 3, you'll remember that your plan serves two distinct purposes: (1) as a roadmap for you to follow, and (2) as a tool to acquire funding from external sources (e.g., bank, private investor, venture capital group, business partner). If individuals are going to invest in you, your company, and your future, they are going to want detailed financial information about your current situation and future projections. Most significantly, they are going to want to know:

- When you anticipate repaying your debt

- How you anticipate repaying your debt

- What financial rewards (e.g., profits, stock, equity interest), if any, they receive in exchange for their investment

- What your revenue and profit projections are

Many of the business plan websites I recommended in Chapter 3 will provide you with detailed information about what type of financial data to include in your business plan. In addition, many will also provide sample forms that you can use to prepare the following financial information, all of which is critical to include in your business plan:

- Statement of Current Financial Needs

- Statement of Projected Financial Needs

- Revenue Projections

- Market and Market Share Projections

- Expense Projections

- Operating Budgets

- Capital Budgets

- Income/Profit Projections

To help you in preparing these often-complex financial documents, be sure to visit the following website where you'll find financial calculators for break-even analysis, cash flow, investment offering, profit margin, and start-up costs. In addition, there are calculators developed specifically for online business ventures to measure conversion rate, return on investment (ROI), and pay-per-click ROI.

- *http://entrepreneur.com/calculators/*

Note that there may be additional financial data, charts, graphs, and tables that you'll want to include in your business plan that are specific to the type of venture you're launching. This is where an accountant and/or financial consultant can be extremely valuable in helping you to formulate a financial plan that not only provides you with realistic projections, but also serves as a marketing tool to entice investors.

Accounting and Financial Management

If you're a small-business owner and are managing your routine bookkeeping, accounting, and financial management functions yourself, then there is no better product on the market than QuickBooks (*www.quickbooks.com*). It is a fully integrated, small-business accounting software program that allows you to manage your accounts payable (what you owe), billings (to customers for products and services), accounts receivable (outstanding payments due to your company), financial reporting, tax reporting, payroll processing, and other critical functions. Most important to you is the fact that it's easy to use.

If you want to move up one step into a more sophisticated software package, then Peachtree Accounting (*www.peachtree.com*) may be your best tool. It has the same basic applications as QuickBooks, but also offers additional enhancements for inventory tracking and order processing, along with 100+ customizable reports.

There are, of course, numerous other accounting and financial-management software programs on the market, many with specialized applications for specific businesses. If you need more than just basic accounting, billing, and financial-reporting capabilities, search the Internet to find software products more suitable for your particular business venture.

Where Does Your Money Come From?

Some businesses generate one type of revenue (or revenue stream) from one particular type of client. The Pampered Chef franchise is a great example of this kind of business, where individual entrepreneurs generate revenue from the cookware products they sell to individual customers within an assigned geographic region. Another example is an online business that sells antique car parts to dealers, collectors, and auto-repair shops nationwide. Another would be a dry-cleaning operation where a small-business owner is providing that particular service to individuals within the local neighborhood.

Other entrepreneurs are much more diversified and may have multiple revenue streams with multiple types of clients. Consider a major bookstore such as Barnes & Noble, which sells books through both retail and online channels, sells to a very broad cross-section of individual and business customers, and, in recent years, has significantly diversified its product lines to include stationery supplies, writing supplies, CDs, DVDs, gifts, calendars, in-store eateries, and so much more. Barnes & Noble was smart and realized that they had a captive audience, both in their stores and online. This allowed them to leverage their brand and successfully introduce new product lines that complemented their core book sales business while capturing new, very profitable revenue streams.

The lesson here is to know where your money comes from. Specifically, ask yourself these questions:

- Where will my revenues come from (revenue streams)?
- What types of customers will I be selling to and/or servicing?
- What types of products or services am I going to sell?
- What advertising channels generate the most clients?
- Which advertising channels generate the most profitable clients?
- Which revenue streams will be the most profitable?

Your answers to these questions are vital to building and managing a successful and profitable entrepreneurial venture. You must truly understand how your business generates each and every dollar that it makes in order to determine which of those dollars are profitable and which are not. You'll then use that information to reconfigure your market focus, realign your advertising dollars, and adjust your promotional efforts to reach out to customers that will generate the highest profit return for your business. Remember, that's what being in business is really all about—making money!

It is important to note that as your business grows and expands, your answers to the previous questions may change dramatically. Remember, businesses are living entities that are constantly changing and re-inventing themselves. As your business transitions over time, your revenue streams and customer mix may also change. Be alert to those changes so that you can quickly and accurately respond, make adjustments in your direction, and ensure your long-term profitability.

CLIENT-CAPTURE ANALYSIS

This chart provides a formula that you can use to evaluate the profitability of each of your revenue streams.

Step #1: Keep a list, database, or Excel spreadsheet of all of your customers and how they found you—the advertising source. The collection and analysis of this data is critical to evaluating the effectiveness and ROI of your marketing, advertising, and promotional dollars. Here's a brief example:

Client Name	Revenue	Advertising Source
George Smith	$1500	NETSHARE
Larry Jordan	$750	Monster.com
Sally Greenblatt	$850	Monster.com
Lester Miles	$1250	NETSHARE
Martin Beck	$600	Yellow Pages
Andrew Meyers	$2500	NETSHARE
Joe Pinco	$500	Yellow Pages
Jane Oscarson	$600	Yellow pages
Amanda Greer	$1250	Client Referral
Randy Ramirez	$1100	Monster.com
Leslie Howard	$850	NETSHARE
Fred Stringer	$1200	Client Referral

Step #2: Calculate the total number of clients and total revenues generated by each advertising source. Here's a brief example using the chart above:

NETSHARE Advertising Source:
Total of 4 clients (Smith, Miles, Meyers, Howard) for a total gross revenue of $6,100.

Step #3: Plug those numbers into the following formula:

$$\frac{\text{Total Revenue from Source}}{\text{Number of Clients from Source}} = \textbf{\textit{Average Revenue per Client}}$$

Average Revenue per Client **-** Cost of Capture **= *Average Net Revenue per Client***

Step #4: Calculate your net revenue per year from each advertising source.

Example 1:

NETSHARE:

Total revenue of $65,200/year ÷ 50 clients/year = **$1,300 average revenue per client**

$1,300 avg. revenue per client − 15% of sale (ad cost)= **$1,108 net revenue per client**

Equivalent to $55,420 net revenue per year (versus $65,200 gross revenue per year)

Example 2:

YELLOW PAGES:

Total revenue of $25,000/year ÷ 50 clients/year = **$500 average revenue per client**

$500 average revenue per client − $24 (advertising cost*) = **$476 net revenue per client**

Equivalent to $23,800 net revenue per year (versus $25,000 gross revenue per year)

NOTE: $24 per client based on $1,200/annual Yellow Pages advertising cost

Example 3:

CLIENT REFERRALS:

Total revenue of $100,000/year ÷ 100 clients/year = $1,000 avg. revenue per client

$1,000 avg. revenue per client − 0% of sale (no ad cost) = **$1,000 net revenue per client**

Equivalent to $100,000 net revenue a year (equivalent to $100,000 gross revenue per year)

*NOTE: Client referrals are obviously your best source for capturing new clients since there is no cost associated with the sale. With most other advertising and referral sources, there will be fixed costs that must be deducted from total annual revenues to capture the true revenue generated by each client and each revenue stream.

Where Does Your Money Go?

Just as important as knowing where your money comes from is knowing where it goes and how it can possibly go so fast! In the previous section, we focused on how your money got in the door; now, we'll focus on how it goes out.

The money that you spend on your business will generally fall into one of the following three categories:

- Start-Up Expenses
- Capital Expenses
- Operating Expenses

Start-up expenses are just that—the costs to launch your business. Some of these expenses may continue and be transferred to ongoing Operating Expenses (e.g., rent, utilities, phones, office supplies, Internet hosting); others will be one-shot expenses (exterior signage and lighting, business license, incorporation and legal fees). To be sure that you capture everything, prepare a financial summary that clearly states all of your anticipated start-up costs and allocates additional dollars for unanticipated expenses. No matter how well you plan, something unexpected will always arise. I guarantee it!

Capital expenses are major asset purchases of such things as buildings and other facilities, land, equipment, automobiles and trucks, and other large-dollar items. You may find that you have some capital expenses required for start-up; other capital expenses may be incurred over the course of time as your business expands. If you're preparing financial forecasts of long-term capital requirements, be sure to calculate in the expected cost increase over the upcoming years.

Operating expenses are the day-to-day costs associated with running your business. Most businesses share certain common expenses (e.g., rent, utilities, phones, computers), yet beyond that, expenses vary dramatically based on the specific type of company that you own. For example, a plastics manufacturer will have significant costs associated with raw materials, packaging, design, quality, warehousing, logistics, and personnel. On the other hand, a graphic-arts design firm may have nothing more than occasional material, software, and technology support costs.

To best understand and control your operating costs, you'll need a monthly budget that will allow you to both forecast your costs and then review your costs to identify and address (hopefully, eliminate) any cost overrides. At first, you may find that your budget requires a great deal of adjustment. Over the long run, however, as your business matures, you'll most often find that you can much more accurately project your costs.

To help you get started, on the next page you'll find a sample monthly budget form that you can adapt for your own use. And, just as with your revenues, your costs can best be recorded and tracked by using QuickBooks (*www.quickbooks.com*) or another accounting software package.

Note that the tax laws governing what can be deducted as business expenses and what cannot are complex. As such, we strongly recommend that you consult an accountant to assist you with all of your monthly, quarterly, and/or annual tax filings payable to federal, state, county, and/or local jurisdictions. It's always best to get it right the first time!

Pricing For Profit

Setting the prices for your products and services will most likely require a great deal of research so that you're certain to establish the right price points for your products, services, geographic markets, customer markets, and more. In order to do this effectively (and profitably), you'll want to carefully consider the following:

- What does your competition charge for the same or similar products and services? What's the high end and what's the low end?

- If you're offering an existing product or service, what do your targeted customers currently pay for that product or service?

- Does your product or service have a value-add that your competitors do not? If so, what do you project that is worth in terms of dollars in the market?

- Who are your targeted customers and do they fall into any particular socioeconomic category?

- Does your specific geographic market impact your pricing? Does it indicate that your pricing should be lower or higher?

- What does it cost to make your product or deliver your service?

- What does it cost to operate your business?

- What is your annual profit objective for your business?

- What is your annual income goal for yourself?

MONTHLY BUDGET

	SAMPLE BUDGET	ACTUAL BUDGET
Rent	$400	$_____
Utilities	$50	$_____
Telephone	$100	$_____
Technology	$100	$_____
Advertising	$200	$_____
Office Supplies	$100	$_____
Banking Fees	$25	$_____
Credit Card Fees	$50	$_____
Professional Fees	$ 50	$_____
Taxes	$250	$_____
Savings	$150	$_____
Health Insurance	$0	$_____
Auto Expense	$0	$_____
_____	$_____	$_____
_____	$_____	$_____
_____	$_____	$_____

TOTAL MONTHLY EXPENSES   **$1,475** $_____

TOTAL ANNUAL EXPENSES

($1,475 x 12) =   **$17,700** $_____

Determining what prices you're going to charge for your products and services is one of the most critical decisions that will impact your profitability. If you don't charge enough, you'll soon discover that you're not making a profit. If you charge too much, you may find that you're pricing yourself right out of the market. It's a fine line to be drawn and one that you must carefully monitor throughout the life of your business.

A colleague of mine once stated that she found that, as her confidence in her abilities increased and as she felt more in control when working with her customers, she was much more comfortable increasing her prices. It was a gradual process, one step at a time, but over the course of several years, she increased her pricing from among the lowest in the industry to among the highest. What's more, her profit margins soared and today she she owns one of the most successful entrepreneurial ventures in her industry.

A word of caution . . . if you're delivering a service, either charge full price or give it away for free. If you discount the price, it will reduce the perceived value of your service in the eyes of your customer.

Services are intangible items that generally can't be seen, touched, smelled, or otherwise experienced. As such, pricing can be more difficult than with products that a potential buyer can pick up, try on, taste, feel, and more. Through these tactile experiences, customers can appreciate the product and better understand its value. As such, when the local Gap store has a sale and their merchandise is discounted, you don't worry that the merchandise is of any lesser value than when it was on the shelf a week ago for twice the retail-selling price.

On the following page—Establishing Your Target Pricing—is a formula to help you define your pricing structure. I've based this pricing formula on the **annual profit goals** for two different businesses: (1) a product business selling customized photographic reproductions, and (2) a service business providing website design. Once the profit goals of each company were established, I subtracted the annual operating costs and forecasted annual product or service volume in order to determine the target price point. In fact, as you'll see, I've demonstrated several different pricing scenarios based on different product volumes for both businesses.

Credit-Card Processing

Almost all businesses today accept credit-card payments for two specific reasons:

ESTABLISHING YOUR TARGET PRICING

Target Pricing Formula:

Step 1.   Annual Profit Goal
   +   Annual Operating Costs
   =   **Total Revenue Objective**

Step 2.   Weekly Product/Service Sales Capacity
   x   48 Working Weeks Per Year
   =   **Annual Product/Service Sales Capacity**

Step 3.   Total Revenue Objective
   ÷   Annual Product/Service Sales Capacity
   =   **Target Price Point**

Profit Goal — $50,000 Net Profit Goal:

Product Company:

$50,000 + $24,000 = $74,000
10 products week x 48 weeks/year = 480 products
$74,000 / 480 products = **$154 per product**

$50,000 + $24,000 = $74,000
5 products/week x 48 weeks/year= 240 products
$74,000/240 products = **$308 per product**

Service Company:

$50,000 + $24,000 = $74,000
25 products week x 48 weeks/year = 1,200 products
$74,000 / 1,200 products = **$61 per product**

$50,000 + $24,000 = $74,000
15 hours x 48 weeks/year= 720 products
$74,000/720 products = **$103 per product**

Profit Goal — $100,000 Net Profit Goal:
(Doubling your profits while only increasing your expenses by 50%)

Product Company:

$100,000 + $34,000 = $134,000
10 products week x 48 weeks/year = 480 products
134,000 / 480 products = **$279 per product**

$100,000 + $34,000 = $134,000
5 products/week x 48 weeks/year= 240 products
$134,000/240 products = **$558 per product**

Service Company:

$100,000 + $34,000 = $134,000
25 hours/week x 48 weeks/year = 1,200 hours
$134,000 / 1,200 hours = **$112 per hour**

$50,000 + $24,000 = $74,000
15 hours x 48 weeks/year= 720 hours
$134,000/720 hours = **$186 per hour**

- It's easy for the customer.

- You can verify that the credit-card funds are good almost instantaneously.

As such, you'll need to set up your business to process credit-card payments. We strongly recommend that you accept both VISA and MasterCard since they are the two most widely used credit cards. In addition, consider adding Discover, American Express, and/or Diner's Club to the mix, all three of which have millions of cardholders worldwide.

Becoming a credit-card merchant requires that you establish a relationship with a credit-card processor. Often, this will be your bank. When you're setting up your business bank account, meet with the Merchant Services Representative from your bank to discuss their credit-card processing services and fees. If your bank cannot assist you or their fees are expensive, then you may consider these alternative, third-party processors:

- **Buyer Zone**   *www.buyerzone.com*

- **Card Service Sales**   *www.cardservicesales.com*

- **Charge It Now**   *www.chargeitnow.com*

- **Charge.com**   *www.charge.com*

- **Commerce Payment Systems**   *www.commercepayment systems.com*

- **Merchant-Accounts**   *www.merchant-accounts.com*

- **Merchant Express**   *www.merchantexpress.com*

- **Merchant Warehouse**   *www.merchantwarehouse.com*

- **PayNet Systems**   *www.paynetsystems.com*

- **PayPal**   *www.paypal.com*

- **Practice Pay Solutions**   *www.practicepaysolutions.com*

- **Transact4Free**   *www.transact4free.com*

Note that there is a fee associated with credit-card processing. Although referred to as a "merchant discount," it is not a discount! Be aware that there will be fees from both the credit-card companies (e.g., VISA, MasterCard) and the credit-card processors (companies that do transaction processing). Fees can range from as low as 1.5% of each transaction to as high as 5% of each transaction. This adds up quickly, so be a cost-effective shopper yourself!

Generating Passive Income

I like to refer to the concept of passive income as *making money while you sleep.* Think about the amount of revenue that Amazon makes every night while the office is closed and the CEO is asleep. The sum is staggering! Or, on a smaller scale, think about the professional speaker who recently authored a book that is now available on his or her website. While that speaker is out of the office on a nationwide speaking tour, individuals are purchasing the book from the website and generating revenue with no effort at all on the part of the speaker.

Both product and service businesses can benefit from passive channels of income, although it's most common with product-driven, online businesses. In these types of businesses, where customers make purchases without any human contact, the revenue potential is extraordinary. However, the concept can also work extremely well for service businesses that can sell auxiliary products (e.g., books, CDs, videos, DVDs, training manuals).

Passive income will not work for each and every business. For example, if your line of work is manufacturing commercial-refrigeration systems, chances are you won't be in a situation to generate passive income and that's okay. The model may not be right for you. Or, if you're an engineering consultant, the only time that you're generating income is when you're at a client site working on a particular project. However, if the opportunity ever presents itself to introduce products and/or services that will generate passive income, I strongly recommend that you do so. As discussed earlier in this chapter, the more revenue streams feeding into your business, the better.

Investing in Yourself

One of the most common mistakes that entrepreneurs make is **not** investing in themselves and **not** saving for their future retirement. This happens for several reasons:

- They do not have extra money to save or invest.
- They are relatively young and do not believe that they need to starting saving for their retirement at such an early age.
- They are confident that their business will, at some point, generate enough money to support their retirement.

- They are planning to sell their business when they're ready to retire, certain that the proceeds will be enough to support them throughout their retirement.

Don't let yourself fall into this trap! Everyone—entrepreneurs included —needs a retirement plan, even if you can only invest a very small amount each week, each month, or each year. Over time, that money will grow —faster than you think—and you'll find that your options for retirement or re-careering are much stronger and more viable.

The most common plans to save for your future are the IRA and the SEP (Self Employment Plan). Talk to your banker, accountant, financial consultant, or investment consultant to learn more about your options and what plan will work best for you and your business.

I cannot stress enough the importance of establishing a savings plan for yourself. Although age 65 may seem a long time from now, and you're certain that your entrepreneurial venture is going to generate millions of dollars, planning for your financial future is a critical function in any business. Don't allow yourself to be short-sighted!

Give It Back ... It's Mine!

The most dreaded word for any entrepreneur is "collections." After you've gone through all the effort to deliver a service or product to your customer, you certainly don't want to have to fight to get your money. But the reality is that you will inevitably be faced with such a situation at one time or another during your entrepreneurial career. It's some of the bad medicine that you'll just have to swallow.

If you're like most entrepreneurs, you've heard about problems that others had when trying to collect customer payments. But you're optimistic and certain that this will never be the case with your business. You're committed to providing consistently high-quality products and top-flight service to each and every one of your customers. Why would they not want to pay you? The thought is inconceivable!

However, there will be situations, no matter what you do, that collecting customer payments may become a problem. As such, you'll want to establish sound financial policies and procedures to expedite payment and reduce the potential for having to work to collect your money.

Following are seven tried-and-true payment policies you should consider implementing into your business:

- **Be careful to whom you extend credit.** Require credit references and be sure to check them out. Set credit limits on customers.

- **No work or product leaves your office, store, warehouse, or home unless it is paid in full.** This practice will work well in certain businesses where payment is rendered by an individual customer or a small-business owner. On the other hand, it may not work as efficiently if you're selling to major corporations that have complex invoice-processing and payment systems.

- **Require prepayment for all products under a certain dollar amount.** For example, do not extend credit for any purchase under $50. Since the cost of collecting on small amounts is high, avoid such credit situations.

- **If you'll be taking credit-card payments, it's essential that you have the technology to support it.** In years past, most credit-card authorizations were handled by telephone. Today, however, the vast majority of processing is computer-based and much easier. Although you'll be responsible for paying the merchant discount—it's actually a fee that's normally 2-3% of each transaction—it's well worth it. Once verified, you know the credit card is good and that the money will be transferred directly into your account.

- **Just as with credit cards, there are also check-verification companies who will authorize the authenticity and value of personal and business checks.** If you'll be taking checks from many unknown customers, this is definitely worth the small expense.

- **Write a letter of agreement or a contract, which lists all the products and services you'll be providing to a customer, schedules, deliverables, fees, and any other relevant information.** Then, have the customer agree to all of the terms and sign the document. This is most appropriate for businesses where you'll be providing ongoing services, delivering a particular project, manufacturing products, or involved in other large-dollar transactions.

- **Don't waste time on bad collections.** If you are having a specific collections problem, you've been trying to collect payment for several weeks or several months, and the amount is rather small, let it go or turn the bad debt over to a collections agency that may be able to recover a portion of the debt. There are probably much better things you could do with your time and effort than to chase someone for a couple of hundred dollars. This is one of the toughest entrepreneurial lessons to learn—*don't take it personally*—even if you feel taken advantage of.

Unfortunately, collections and bad debts are a part of almost every business. To minimize your exposure, implement sound business practices to reduce your risk and limit your liabilities.

The IRS: Every Entrepreneur's Nightmare

Being in business for yourself means that you're going to have to pay taxes to the IRS. Most people cringe when you mention the IRS, but that doesn't have to be the case. There are, of course, regulations that you must comply with and tax documents that you must file. However, as with any other business, the IRS has made it much easier with their online Tax Center. Here are some of the most useful and informative links for entrepreneurs:

Tax Information for Start-Up Businesses
There are specific tax issues that impact small-business owners and other self-employed individuals:

http://www.irs.gov/businesses/small/index.html

Business Start-Up Checklist
The IRS provides an excellent, step-by-step resource to help individuals plan and launch start-up businesses:

http://www.irs.gov/businesses/small/article/0,,id=98810,00.html

Structuring Your New Venture
One of the first decisions you'll need to make when starting your business is what type of structure to use, which involves critical tax and legal considerations:

http://www.irs.gov/businesses/small/article/0,,id=98359,00.html

Employer ID Number

All businesses must have a federal tax number, known as a Federal Employer Identification Number (EIN):

http://www.irs.gov/businesses/small/article/0,,id=98350,00.html
http://www.irs.gov/businesses/small/article/0,,id=102767,00.html

Business Taxes

There will be different IRS forms to file and taxes to pay based on the specific type of business that you operates:

http://www.irs.gov/businesses/small/article/0,,id=98966,00.html

Tax Law Changes

It's important that you remain up-to-date on changes to relevant tax laws and regulations:

http://www.irs.gov/formspubs/article/0,,id=97397,00.html

Disaster Site Web Link

If your business has experienced a disaster, you may be eligible for tax savings and credits:

http://www.irs.gov/newsroom/article/0,,id=147085,00.html
http://www.irs.gov/newsroom/article/0,,id=108362,00.html

IRS Forms and Publications

There will be numerous IRS forms and publications that you'll need over the life of your business:

http://www.irs.gov/formspubs/index.html

Electronic Tax Filing
http://www.irs.gov/efile/article/0,,id=118520,00.html
http://www.eftps.gov/

Strategic Financial Concepts for the Entrepreneur

Following are five critically important strategic concepts about business finance, accounting, and money management that each and every entrepreneur must know. What's more, not only must you understand these concepts, they should become a key component in your roadmap to entrepreneurial success.

Strategy #1: Get Professional Guidance

As I commented at the beginning of this chapter, unless you happen to be an accounting or finance professional with skills in managing money, controlling costs, developing budgets, negotiating credit lines, and more, then hire an expert. These individuals can be one of the most valuable contributors to your success throughout the entire life of your business.

My motto … *Thank goodness for accountants and bookkeepers!* Most entrepreneurs are much better at making money rather than controlling money. The real challenge, therefore, is knowing what to do with the money that you do make, how to manage it, how to save it, and what each entry on your financial statement really means to your success.

Strategy #2: Learn How Your Money Works

Let me share a little story . . . I had owned my first business for three years. However, I had struggled financially for all three years and was ready to throw in the towel. I called my accountant and we met on a Friday afternoon, during which time I announced my intention to bankrupt the corporation and go get a job. It had to be easier! The shrewd business advisor that he was, my accountant sent me home for the weekend to think things through before I made any final decision.

By the time we met again on Monday, my head had cleared, I'd let go of some of the stress, and I had reaffirmed my commitment to see my business through to success and profitability. It was on that day that I made the commitment to myself that I was going to learn about my money, how it worked, where it came from, where it went, and so much more. From that day forward, everything was different and since that time, I've experienced strong profit margins each and every year. It took me a while to learn the lessons; hopefully, this book will make your lessons a bit easier.

Strategy #3: Things Will Forever Change

Accept the fact that businesses are cyclical and that it is unrealistic to expect that your business will be profitable each and every day of its existence. Rather, the norm is more likely to be feast or famine. You'll have a couple of great months where you make a lot of money, only to be followed by several months where business really slows down. Then, just as you begin to think that your customers have deserted you forever, the phones will start ringing, orders will come pouring in, and you'll be overwhelmed. As an entrepreneur, your worklife will never be equalized and the sooner you accept this fact, the happier your entrepreneurial career will be.

Strategy #4: Build Your Referral Network

Focus your efforts on building your stream of customer referrals—referrals from other businesses, referrals from past customers, and referrals from your network of contacts. There are two great things about referrals: (1) they are pre-sold on you, your business, your products, and/or your services, and (2) there is no cost to capture them. As I demonstrated with my Client Capture Analysis Formula, earlier in this chapter, most customers have a fixed cost of capture (e.g., advertising costs, referral fees, promotional costs). Referred customers come to you for free!

Strategy #5: Technology is a Valuable Tool

And, finally, remember that accounting software is your friend! As stated earlier in this chapter, I recommend QuickBooks as the preferred software for small business owners. However, there are other similar products on the market that you may elect to use, based on personal preferences and the recommendations of your accountant or financial consultant.

7

One Day at a Time:
Managing Your Daily Business Operations

THIS CHAPTER PROVIDES an overview of some of the typical, day-to-day business operations for which most entrepreneurs are responsible. Obviously, specific operations will vary from one business entity to another. For example, the daily functions within a two-person auto-repair service business will vary dramatically from the daily functions within a 200-person manufacturing operation which, again, are substantially different than the daily functions required to run a retail store.

This chapter is divided into several key sections that will address the following critical business and operating functions:

- Policy and Procedure Development
- Staffing and Human Resources Management
- Purchasing and Materials Management
- Quality Management
- "Corporate" Management

All of the other core business functions—business planning, sales, marketing, finance, technology, and customer-relationship management—have been addressed in the previous chapters because of the detailed information that each new entrepreneur must know.

Policy and Procedure Development

One of the biggest mistakes that many entrepreneurs make is not writing things down. This is particularly true of the small-business entrepreneur who either works alone or has just a few employees. These individuals often keep a great deal of information about their business operations in their heads. They know what needs to be done, they either do it themselves or have trained others to do it, and their time is very limited. As such, they never allocate the time and effort that is necessary to document all of their business processes.

Although many entrepreneurs can function quite effectively in this mode, there are dangers in doing so! Suppose, for example, that you unexpectedly become ill and are not able to work for a few days or a few weeks. What will happen to your business then? Will your employees know how to do what needs to be done? Will they be able to find what they need? Will they know how to manage and control your business operations in your absence? Or, what if you want to sell your business at some point in the future? Do you have all your procedures and processes documented for a potential new owner? Will they understand how your business operates?

> *One of the biggest mistakes entrepreneurs make is not writing things down.*

Unfortunately, for many entrepreneurs, the answers to those questions are no for they have never formally documented how their business operates. In turn, the business becomes entirely dependent on them—the entrepreneurial owner—and they must be there each and every day to provide hands-on management for all aspects of their operation. That means no sick days, no vacations, and no time away from the business.

At first, when you're overly enthusiastic about your new venture, your 24/7 work schedule might seem okay. However, trust me when I tell you that, over the long haul, you will need to take some time off, re-energize your batteries, clear your head, and even be sick. It happens to the best of us!

To ensure that your business is able to operate in your absence, it is critical that you document every function, from mixing ingredients for your bakery, to scheduling shipments of your electronic components, to processing customer invoices and payments (and a few hundred other things!). As such, I strongly urge that you start documenting everything today by **creating a**

comprehensive operations manual that includes step-by-step instructions for handling each and every function within your organization (e.g., finance, accounting, human resources, information technology, sales, marketing, customer-relationship management, purchasing, inventory control, logistics, shipping and receiving, quality, manufacturing, product inspection, product development, service delivery...the list goes on and on).

Although this may seem like a daunting task, the Internet provides a wealth of resources that can make writing operating manuals easier and more efficient. Here are a few select resources—some for free and others for a fee—you can consider using to help you put together a top-notch manual that can guide you and your employees in managing your daily business operations:

- *http://store.bizmanualz.com/products/policies_procedures.html? src=G_N12_business_manual&gclid=CMTVvfzQ5oYCFQFZHgod kEkG_w*

- *http://www.templatezone.com/employee-handbook.php*

- *www.allbusiness.com/operations/3357-1.html*

- *www.business.com/directory/human_resources/workforce_manage-ment/employee_manuals_and_policies/*

- *www.copedia.com/*

- *www.frandocs.com/Operations%20Manual%20550%20pages.htm*

Another huge benefit of documenting your business processes is consistency in operations. Once you've outlined the step-by-step procedures for a specific business function, then there are never any questions about how to do it and everyone does it the same way. Consistency then leads to gains in productivity and efficiency which, in turn, will improve your bottom-line profitability.

Everything you do in your business, for your business, to your business, and about your business ultimately does impact the bottom-line—even something as simple as documenting your general bookkeeping or hiring procedures.

Staffing and Human Resources Management

Entrepreneurs often don't play well with others! In fact, many prefer to work in isolation when possible, alone with their thoughts, ideas, projects, tools, and more. If you always plan to operate as a solo entrepreneur, and you're happy with your business, satisfying your customers, and making money, great! However, the vast majority of entrepreneurs will need to hire, train, mentor, supervise, evaluate, and pay others to work for them.

If you have strong management and leadership skills, then you may thoroughly enjoy the personnel component of your business. If, on the other hand, you are happy to be alone with your work, managing others can prove to be a more difficult task. You'll find that your workday is often focused on solving your employees' needs, responding to their questions, helping them with their projects, handling things when they're unexpectedly absent ... you get the picture. With one or two employees, it's usually not a big deal. However, as your staff grows and grows, be aware that your job is going to change dramatically. No longer will you be working in your business; rather, you'll be working on your business as you manage your team.

Here are some essential questions to ask yourself as you build and grow your business:

- When do I anticipate that I will need to hire employees? Right now? In six months? Next year?

- What will I need my employees to do? Sales? Customer service? Manufacturing? Engineering?

- What are the key skills I need in qualified candidates? Professional skills? Management skills? Soft skills?

- Do I need full-time or part-time employees?

- Do I want to hire employees or contractors? Temporary or permanent?

- How am I going to pay my employees and/or my contractors? Hourly? Annual salary? Bonus, commission, or incentive plan?

- Where can I find contractors?

- What benefits, if any, am I going to provide to my employees?

- What days do I need my personnel to work? What hours?

- Do I need to have contracts with my employees? With my management team?

- Do I need to develop an employee handbook?

Note that early-stage entrepreneurs often waver between hiring employees versus contractors. Consider the fact that with employees you have more control—over what they do each day, when they do it, and how they do it. With contractors, you pay them to do a job and you often step away. Furthermore, contractors, although they may be more expensive than employees on a per-hour basis, are often less expensive in the long run since you do not have to pay matching taxes and benefits. If you're uncertain as to the type of personnel you need to bring into your organization, I recommend that you consult an accountant who can provide detailed information on the laws and regulations governing all classes of personnel.

Purchasing and Materials Management

Purchasing and materials management requirements will vary dramatically from one type of business to another. A small graphic-design shop will have minimal material needs while a mid-size clothing manufacturer will, most likely, be purchasing from scores of vendors and will need a complex inventory-planning and control system.

Ask yourself the following questions:

- What do I need to buy to operate my business? At start-up? On an ongoing basis?

- Do I need to purchase capital equipment or other fixed assets? Where can I purchase them? What will it cost?

- Do I need to purchase consumables and/or raw materials? From where and for how much?

- Do I need to set up purchasing agreements/contracts/accounts with suppliers I will be using regularly?

- What are each supplier's payment terms and conditions?

- Where and how am I going to store raw materials? Any special requirements?

- What inventory management system am I going to use? Why?

- How will I manage my ongoing purchasing and know what needs to be ordered and when?

If you own a business with significant materials requirements, be certain to devote adequate time and effort to identifying cost-effective suppliers.

The tighter you control your expenses, the lower your costs will be and the stronger your profit margins.

Quality Management

Whether you own a product-manufacturing business, an automotive-service company, or a technology-consulting firm, quality is critical to your long-term success and profitability. When your customers do business with you, they anticipate that you will deliver high-quality services and/products. It's that simple. They do an excellent job in their jobs, and they expect you to do the same.

Introducing quality-control and management systems is essential for each and every business. To get started, consider these important questions:

- What are my specific quality objectives?

- What do I have to do to achieve those objectives? What are my step-by-step plans?

- How am I going to measure my internal quality performance? What systems? What metrics? What analysis methods?

- What will I do to reach out to my customers to obtain their feedback about the quality of my products and/or services?

- How am I going to translate that analytical information into actionable plans and processes?

- Is it important that my company earn any specific quality certifications, such as ISO? Will these certifications strengthen my market position and help capture new customers? Are they essential for certain customers?

- If my company requires it, what will it cost to create a formal quality-management process/organization? Who will manage it?

"Corporate" Management

Whether or not you're incorporated, there are several critical "corporate" business-management functions you will want/need to attend to:

- Do you need a Board of Directors or a Board of Advisors? If so, who will you invite to join the Board and what is that person's particular expertise?

- Whom, if anyone, are you responsible for reporting to? Board of Directors? Investors? Shareholders? Other stakeholders?

- When and how will you report to them? On a regular basis? As needs and problems may arise?

- Have you developed a strategic business plan? How often will you review and update that plan? Who will assist with that function?

- Have you developed your administrative systems and procedures? Your process for annual reporting? Your organizational hierarchy and infrastructure?

- Do you need a corporate safety, security, and disaster preparedness plan to protect and secure people? Facilities? Technology? Equipment?

- If you create intellectual property, how will you protect those assets?

- Do you have a long-term business-succession plan for who will take over the company when you depart?

- Have you created the checks and balances to ensure that you meet all regulatory and licensing requirements? Tax filing deadlines?

- Have you assembled your business support team of advisors and mentors?

Problem-Solving Made Simple

One of the greatest challenges facing every entrepreneur is his or her ability to solve problems. Some of these problems may be anticipated, such as changes in market conditions, customer base, technology requirements, and more. Others, however, may be totally unexpected, such as funding sources that have dried up, changes in regulatory and licensing requirements, obsolete equipment, and unanticipated staffing changes.

When these problems arise, all too many entrepreneurs find themselves floundering, uncertain of which direction to take or how to resolve the situation. To help you with your problem-solving challenges, here is a four-step process that is guaranteed to work each and every time.

- **Step 1: Define the problem, challenge, situation, or obstacle in as much detail as possible.** How did this problem arise? What/who caused this problem? Did you do something that caused this to happen? Were you not paying attention to something that was important? Have you experienced this problem before and, if so, did your solution work then? Will the same solution work now?

- **Step 2: Imagine all the alternatives, no matter how costly, nontraditional, or detailed they may be.** This is a creative brainstorming process that encourages you to look at all of your options—no matter how realistic they are or are not. This challenges you to think outside the box and come up with unique solutions that can expediently resolve the issues at hand.

- **Step 3: Narrow down and prioritize your choices based on expenses, resources, consequences, and more.** Look closely at each of your alternatives, determine which are the most reasonable to pursue, and then clearly define all necessary resources to accomplish your objective.

- **Step 4: Select a solution and commit to it.** Once you've chosen your course of action, stick with it. If, after careful review and analysis, you selected what you consider to be the most reasonable solution, commit yourself and your business to it 100%. Don't allow yourself to second-guess your decisions (unless, of course, your solution proves to be totally incorrect).

The next time you're facing a business challenge, try using this process. I guarantee you'll be amazed at how quickly you can reach the right decision!

Planning for the Future

At some point—whether next week, next year, or 20 years from now—it will most likely be time for you to move on and leave your business behind. Generally, you'll make this decision for one of the following reasons:

- **You've had enough!** Your business has not performed as well as you had expected, it's been a financial struggle, and you're frustrated and unhappy. If that's the case, you may determine that it's time to leave the business behind and move on to something that is more fulfilling and more lucrative. In this situation, you may just "close the doors" and walk away, realizing that you've gained new experience and skills while learning some valuable lessons that should serve you well throughout your entire career.

- **You decide to sell your business.** If you've been successful but are now ready to leave the business to pursue other opportunities, you may decide it's time to sell. You can either try to sell it yourself or work with a business broker who can help you market your business and negotiate the best sales transaction. If you're looking for a quick and easy way to sell the business, then selling it yourself may be the answer since you can probably make this happen much faster than if you work with a business broker. If you work with a business broker, the sales cycle may be longer and you'll have to give the broker a percentage of the proceeds. However, in this situation, the proceeds are often higher since your broker should have a great deal of experience in transacting these arrangements and can most likely negotiate a higher selling price.

- **Your business is acquired.** Although you may not have had any intentional plans to sell your business, the reality may be that you've created something valuable and someone else wants it. We should all be so lucky! In this scenario, you may be approached by either an individual or a company interested in acquiring your business. This may be a competitor who wants to capture your customers and revenues, and eliminate you from the competitive landscape; it may be a new entrepreneur who wants to acquire an existing venture rather than start his or her own from scratch; or it may be a venture-capital or investment firm that sees great opportunity and wants to expand your business and move it to the next level. Whatever the circumstance, if you're fortunate enough to be approached for acquisition, you'll most likely want to give it serious consideration, take the money if it's a good offer, and walk away.

Only you can make that decision based on "where" you are in your life and how profitable the opportunity may be.

- **You turn over the leadership** of your business to someone else—a relative, a business partner, an employee, or another individual. If this has been your goal all along, you most likely will have developed a formal succession plan—a step-by-step plan that will allow another individual to gradually move into your position and take over the leadership of the company. This is often the case in family-owned enterprises where the parent grooms the adult child to take over the business one day. This will often allow you to continue generating income from the business despite the fact that you are no longer "working" in the business.

- **You experience something unexpected and have to move on.** You personal life can get in the way of your professional life and often there's nothing you can do about it. You may have an elderly parent who requires 24/7 care, a spouse who's been relocated and your business is not transportable, a child in need of full-time attention, an illness that requires you to slow down or stop working altogether, or any one of a number of other life-changing situations. If this is the case, you will most likely have some difficult business decisions to make, but, ultimately, your health and your family must come first.

Entrepreneurial Lifestyle Management

One of the greatest challenges that every entrepreneur faces is the infamous issue of work/life balance. This can be a huge struggle for many entrepreneurs who have invested themselves, their effort, their expertise, and their finances into building a successful venture. Hand-in-hand with that investment comes intense demands on your time—to operate and manage your business, fulfill your customer obligations, meet project deadlines, upgrade your technologies, introduce new customer-management procedures, investigate new markets, design sales brochures, manage accounting and finance, negotiate with suppliers, control your inventory, and so much more. The number of tasks for which you will be responsible is never-ending, so get used to it!

One of the hardest lessons for me to learn has been to simply walk out of the office at the end of each day. I'm a task master and always want to get everything done. My goal has always been to finish each day with a clean desk so that when I come in the following morning, I'm fresh and ready to start anew. What I've learned, however, is that's virtually impossible.

The demands on you, your time, and your energy will be never-ending, and you'll never get everything done. Somehow, you have to learn how to deal with that and find a way to feel fulfilled at the end of each day and ready to tackle the next day, despite the fact that your desk will be piled high and the stack of phone messages and emails may be overwhelming. It's the price that many of us "pay" to be entrepreneurs.

Be sure to take the time to carefully and thoroughly read Chapter 9, *How Well Do You Juggle?* In that chapter, you'll find lots of valuable information and "tricks of the trade" about how to manage your time, increase your productivity, improve your efficiency, and much more. Are you a "chunker" or task master like me? Do you have the right systems in place to expedite your business operations? Have you hired the right people? Do you have the best technologies? All of these items and more will enhance your ability to effectively manage your time and optimize your productivity.

As entrepreneurs, we often forget how critically important it is to take care of ourselves. Without you, your business will have nothing—particularly if you're a small-business owner who's involved in virtually everything that happens at your business. With that said, it is imperative that you find ways to pull yourself away from your business and invest your energies in your personal life. You simply cannot sustain a 24/7 work schedule forever. Eventually, it will take its toll on you, your family, and your business. Focus on finding a way to blend your personal and professional lives. If balance isn't a reality for you, perhaps work/life blend is a more realistic possibility.

All too many entrepreneurs burn out from exhaustion. They find that they're simply in over their heads and cannot continue to work at such a rigorous pace. Their family barely recognizes them, their friends haven't seen them in ages, and they have no real quality of life outside of work. Bottom-line, that's not healthy for anyone.

To ensure that you're living a fulfilled entrepreneurial life, be certain that the following are on the top of your list of priorities:

- Sleep (more than three hours a day is highly recommended!)
- Nutritious food (that does NOT include a Big Mac!)
- Exercise (more than just walking to and from your car!)
- Friends (yes, you still do have them!)

- Family time (over time, they'll come to know you again!)
- Entertainment (when was the last time you saw a movie or went to an autumn festival?)
- Vacations (I remember one from 2004!)

If you don't take care of yourself, no one else will. Somehow, despite all of your entrepreneurial demands, you must find the time to devote to things other than work. In fact, it's often these outside interests, activities, and people that will often give you renewed energy and enthusiasm for yourself and your business. Don't get so immersed in your company that everything else around you falls away. That's too high a price to pay!

8

Technology:
It's a Tool, Not a Solution

R EAD THE TITLE OF THIS CHAPTER again—*Technology: It's a Tool; Not a Solution.* This is an extremely critical concept for all business entrepreneurs who think that if they implement technology, it will solve all of their problems and make their operations run like clockwork. If it were only that easy!

Technology does have many benefits and will indeed help your business operate more efficiently, more productively, more consistently, and, perhaps, more profitably. In fact, many technologies will allow you to streamline, accelerate, and enhance the overall performance of your organization. However, it is not a solution in and of itself. It is simply a tool that, when used appropriately, can add measurable value to your business venture.

The only time that technology is a solution is if your primary business is the delivery of technology solutions. Perhaps you've launched a networking-solutions company, a website-design firm, an enterprise-solutions consulting group, or a GPS software-design company. If so, I'll assume that you have expert technology skills and qualifications, and if that's the case, you may find that the information in this chapter is below your skill level and can be quickly skimmed.

For everyone else reading this book, this chapter provides extremely valuable information about the technology tools that you'll need to launch and then effectively manage your business organization and all of its critical operating components. I've attempted to give you a broad overview of some of the most common tools that should be a part of your technology toolkit.

Be advised, however, that technologies are changing each and every day, and that this information was the best information available at the time that I wrote this book. I strongly recommend that you do your own research to identify any newer technologies that may add value to your operations.

The Entrepreneur's Technology Toolkit

Technology needs vary dramatically from one business to another depending on several critical factors:

- Specific type of business or industry

- Specific products and/or services that you deliver

- Method of delivery

- Personal level of technical proficiency

- Financial assets to acquire technology

Some entrepreneurs may have very basic technology requirements. For example, a small, home-based tailoring business may only need Microsoft Office and QuickBooks to handle all of their functions. On the other end of the spectrum, a toy design and manufacturing company may require a wealth of technology tools (e.g., Microsoft Office, Excel, QuickBooks, CAD, GPS, manufacturing-automation tools, supply-chain management technology tools).

To help you determine which tools you need and why, this chapter outlines some of the most common software products on the market that will help you build, manage, and control your business operations. If you need help in understanding any of the technical language and terms used throughout the chapter, be sure to visit one of the following online technology dictionaries. They are wonderful tools and a critical resource for every non-tech entrepreneur.

- **Glossarist**   *www.glossarist.com/glossaries/ technology*

- **High-Tech Dictionary**   *www.computeruser.com/resources/
  dictionary/dictionary.html*

- **Tech Dictionary**   *www.techdictionary.com*

- **TechEncyclopedia**   *www.techweb.com/encyclopedia*

- **Technology Dictionary**   *www.techdict.org*

- **Webopedia**   *www.webopedia.com*

- **Whatis.com**   *http://whatis.techtarget.com*

Office-Automation Tools

Without a doubt, Microsoft Office is the most widely used and accepted office-software package available on the market. As such, it is the obvious recommendation if for no other reason than the facilitation of document transmission from one person to another, without the hassle of software incompatibility.

What's more, Microsoft Office provides a complete software package that meets most common business requirements. When you purchase Office, you get:

- **Microsoft Office** (for word processing)

- **Microsoft Excel** (for spreadsheets)

- **Microsoft Outlook** (for email)

- **Microsoft PowerPoint** (for presentations)

- **Microsoft Explorer** (for Internet browsing)

There are several different versions of Microsoft Office so you'll need to visit the Microsoft website (*www.microsoft.com*) to learn more about each and select the one that is right for you and your business.

If, for some reason, you prefer not to use Microsoft Office, you should do an extensive Internet search to identify software tools that will be more appropriate to your business. In fact, there are thousands of software products designed specifically for different types of business and different industries (e.g., dental software, manufacturing software, logistics software, association software, customer-service software).

Another great addition to your office-automation tools is Adobe Acrobat (*http://www.adobe.com/products/acrobat*), a family of products that allows you to create and exchange documents, and tailor the security of a file in order to maintain its integrity. Often referred to as .pdf files, Adobe documents let you capture and view robust information—from any application on any computer system—and share it with anyone worldwide. What's more, Adobe has customized applications for virtually every profession, from manufacturing, construction, and engineering to finance and beyond.

Accounting and Financial-Management Tools

If you're a small-business owner and are managing your routine bookkeeping, accounting, and financial-management functions yourself, then there is no better product on the market than QuickBooks (*www.quickbooks.com*). It is a fully integrated, small-business accounting software program that allows you to manage your accounts payable, billings, accounts receivable, financial reporting, tax reporting, payroll processing, and other critical functions. Most important to you is the fact that it's easy to use.

If you want to move up one step into a more sophisticated software package, then Peachtree Accounting (*www.peachtree.com*) may be your best tool. It has the same basic applications as QuickBooks, but also offers additional enhancements for inventory tracking and order processing, along with 100+ customizable reports.

There are, of course, countless other accounting and financial-management software programs on the market, many with specialized applications for specific businesses. If you need more than just basic accounting, billing, and financial-reporting capabilities, search the Internet to find software products more suitable for your particular business venture.

Note that although your Microsoft Office software does include Microsoft Excel, that application is not for general accounting. Rather, Excel is a software program designed to produce financial spreadsheets as part of your total financial-management program.

Credit-Card Processing

One of the most critical things you can do to ensure that your business is generating revenues is to make it easy for your customers to pay! And, in today's world, there is little that is easier than credit cards. In generations past, people rarely used credit cards, except for unanticipated expenses and emergencies. Today, however, with all of the incentives that companies offer, people are using credit cards on a regular basis to pay for everything, from gas to college tuition.

What's more, it has become increasingly difficult to write checks. Many companies don't take personal checks, others don't take out-of-state checks, and still others require extensive documentation and verification to even process your check. Frankly, it's easier and faster to charge, whether you're purchasing a shirt at your local retail store or buying books from an online vendor.

I examined this issue as well as identified third-party processors on page 126.

Database Management

Managing your database of contacts—customers, prospects, suppliers, contractors, colleagues, and more—is an essential component of every successful business. Without information and knowledge, you have little on which to build, expand, and succeed. Therefore, it is critical that you develop an easy-to-manage, easy-to-use system to establish, maintain, and update your contact network.

Fortunately, technology has provided numerous tools that you can use for database development and management. The most widely used software programs include:

- **ACT**   *www.act.com*
- **Computer Associates**   *www.ca.com*
- **FileMaker**   *www.filemaker.com*
- **IBM**   *www.ibm.com/db2*
- **Microsoft Access**   *www.microsoft.com*
- **Quest Central**   *www.quest.com*

Note that the information you have in these databases will also be important when you're communicating with these individuals and/or companies about new products, new services, changes in business operations, special promotions, and much more. You'll read all about this in an upcoming section on Email-Broadcast Campaigns.

Email

Here's the reality . . . you can't be in business in this day and age if you don't have email. No matter what type of business you have, people are going to want to communicate with you via email. These communications may differ radically in their nature—an inquiry from a prospective customer for more information about one of your specific products, a product catalog from a supplier, an invoice from your long-distance telephone-service provider … the list goes on and on.

Before you even open your business for business, it's essential that you have your email in place and ready to go. In fact, it's likely that you'll be sending out email announcements about the opening of your business, in addition to the more traditional grand-opening activities you might engage in (e.g., advertisements, press releases, special events).

You cannot be in business if you don't have email.

There are two important decisions that you'll have to make about your email technology. First, you'll need to decide which email-software program you're going to use and, second, you'll need to establish an email account for your business.

Your first decision—which email-software program to select—is often a no-brainer. A huge percentage of entrepreneurs and businesses that use Microsoft Office also use Microsoft Outlook or Outlook Express as their email program of choice. It's easy to use, efficient, and has good basic applications. In fact, you can consider it the industry standard.

There are, of course, other email programs available on the market including Eudora (*www.eudora.com*) and Thunderbird (*http://www.mozilla. com/thunderbird/*). It doesn't matter which email program you use as long as it works for you!

The second important decision you'll need to make is what email account you want to use. Basically, you have three choices:

- **Paid email account** with any one of thousands of email service companies (*www.aol.com, www.msn.com, www.comcast.net, www.bellsouth.net, www.verizon.net, www.netzero.net*)

- **Free email account** (e.g., *www.gmail.com, www.hotmail.com, www.inbox.com, www.goowy.com, www.care2email.com, http:// mail.lycos.com/lycos/Index.lycos*)

- **Website email account** (e.g., *www.impactpublications.com, www.wendyenelow.com, www.travelocity.com, www.hirevets- first.gov, www.harvard.edu, www.redcross.org, www.traffic- wave.net*)

Bottom-line, free email accounts are not my recommendation for entrepreneurs and small business owners. Most of these names are quite recognizable —as free accounts—and, therefore, may communicate the wrong message. If you don't have $20 a month or so to pay for your email account, how successful is your business? My advice: spend the money and create the right perception.

Another important consideration for effectively managing your email is an autoresponder. Just as its name implies, autoresponders are capable of responding to your incoming email messages when you're not available (e.g., holidays, vacations, sabbaticals, illnesses). When you set up an autoresponder, every incoming email will be answered with your pre-scripted message. That way, people know you've received the message, but you're unavailable to respond at the moment. A typical autoresponder message might read something like this:

> "Hi. Thanks for contacting me. I'm on vacation the week of August 14 and will be back in the office on Monday, August 20. I'll respond to your email message then. Thanks and have a great day!"

If you do a search on the Internet, you will find the numerous companies providing autoresponder capabilities. You can either use a software program that has the function or, for a minimal fee, use an autoresponder service that will post these messages whenever you need them.

And, finally, every outgoing email you send will have what is known as a signature line at the bottom of the message. Basically, a signature line includes your full name, company name, and contact information (usually mailing address, phone and fax numbers, email address, and website). Here's an example:

John R. Edwards, P.E.
Product Design & Manufacturing Engineer
Product Solutions Group, Inc.
222 Main Street, Suite 1100, Toledo, OH 43282
Phone: 216-555-2100
Fax: 216-555-2112
Email: jrdpe@psg.com
Website: www.psg.com

By including all of this information, you're quickly accomplishing two important things:

- Validating that you're a real company.

- Making it easy for people to get in touch with you.

Email Broadcast Campaigns

Staying in touch with your customers and communicating with your prospects are always important functions for every business. In years past, however, this was often a time-consuming and expensive activity that few entrepreneurs and small-business owners attended to. Thanks to today's new technologies, you now have the capability to produce email broadcast campaigns.

Simply put, email broadcasts allow you to instantly transmit large numbers of emails with just the push of a button. These messages can be sent to your entire customer database or just a select group from your database, as well as to lists of prospects and others with whom you want to stay in touch on a regular basis. They're a wonderful addition to every business owner's toolkit.

You can use email broadcast campaigns to produce and transmit:

- Newsletters

- Marketing communications

- New-product announcements

- Special offers and promotions

- Press releases and media kits

- Conference and meeting information

- Product literature

- Catalogs (using website links)

The type of information you can send via email broadcast is virtually unlimited.

If you use Microsoft Office, it is possible to produce email broadcast campaigns using Outlook Express. In fact, you can also use other email-software programs. However, the technology underlying these systems was not intended for this type of application and, as such, takes a lot time to transmit.

To respond to the increasing demand for email broadcast capabilities, several companies have emerged onto the scene to meet this specific need.

Now, not only can you easily and quickly produce email campaigns, these programs also provide capabilities for managing your database of contacts, tracking the number of people who open your email message, imbedding website links into email campaigns and tracking the number of hits, and much more. They're not very expensive and well worth the investment!

- **Bronto**   *http://bronto.com*
- **Campaigner Pro**   *www.campaignerpro.com*
- **Constant Contact**   *www.constantcontact.com*
- **ElectroSoft**   *www.electrosoft.com*
- **Exact Target**   *http://email.exacttarget.com/ETWeb/default.aspx*
- **IntelliContact**   *www.intellicontact.com*
- **Stream Send**   *www.streamsend.com*

All of these companies provide similar services, although fees do vary so I recommend that you consult them all to determine which one is right for you and your business. Personally, I prefer Constant Contact, which is the most widely used of all of these services.

One word of caution . . . think about the amount of spam that you receive in your email inbox daily. Not only is it annoying, but it's perceived as unprofessional. Make sure that all of the individuals in your email database are individuals who want to be in touch with you and want to receive information from you. Don't become a spammer!

Websites and E-Commerce Tools

Being in business today means having an online presence and identity, and, for most businesses, that will be your company's website. It will be the place where people can find you and your business, learn about your products and services, read about your credentials, get in touch with you, place orders, make purchases, and so much more.

Building a website can range dramatically in its complexity, from a very simple and short website (*www.google.com*) to an extremely lengthy, detailed, and technologically sophisticated site (*www.att.com*). What you decide to do and how you do it will depend entirely on what you want your website to do for you and your business. Consider your options:

- **Websites designed as marketing tools** to solicit new business (e.g., *www.merrymaids.com*, where you can search your local region to find a Merry Maids service provider in your area).

- **Websites designed as information tools** to disseminate information, generally to an established customer base (e.g., *www. ieee.org*, the professional-association website for the Institute of Electrical and Electronic Engineers; used to provide membership information and deliver member services).

- **Websites with e-commerce capabilities** (e.g., *www.amazon. com* where you can transact purchases).

Your website can be used to accomplish any one of the above, any combination, or all three as appropriate to your specific business venture. You'll find that most websites are designed to both capture new customers while providing service/support to their existing customer base. Obviously, item #3, e-commerce capabilities, is only relevant to companies that actually sell their products or services online. For more information about e-commerce and "shopping carts" (the technology used to shop and pay), visit these websites:

- *http://checkout.google.com*
- *www.business.com*
- *www.buyerzone.com*
- *www.ezimerchant.com*
- *www.goemerchant.com*
- *www.instantproducts.com*
- *www.monstercommerce.com*
- *www.netstores.com*
- *www.storefront.net*
- *www.volusion.com*
- *www.zencart.com*

Once you've made the above decision, you will have completed step #1 in what will be an entire process to develop your website. And, as with any other project, you need a step-by-step plan to guide you throughout the process. Broken down into simple terms, these are the decisions that you'll need to make in order to establish your website and build your Web presence.

- What do you want your website to do? (Step #1 above)
- What do you want your website to look and feel like (colors and design)?
- What information are you going to include on your website and who is going to write it?
- Who is going to do the technical programming for your website?
- Who is going to do the design for your website?
- What type of navigation do you want to use on your website?
- Who is going to do your website marketing for you?
- Who is going to register your website with the major search engines?
- What other sites are you going to link to from your website?

These are all critically important questions to ask yourself before you even get started. Once you have your plan in place, you can then begin to assemble the technical and people resources that you'll need in order to transition your website from concept into reality.

I strongly recommend that you consult with a website designer, unless you happen to have excellent technical skills yourself and think that you can tackle this project alone. For most entrepreneurs and small-business owners, other than those in the technology arena, hiring a professional to do this for you will pay for itself over and over. Just as with any other profession, there are tricks of the trade that only insiders know! Your website will be a critical component of your business, so be sure that it is done well and accurately represents your company and your business lines.

If you do decide to create your own website, go to *www.templatemonster. com* where you'll find thousands of website templates for under $75.00. Or, consider the following software programs that are designed for ease in use:

- *www.adobe.com/products/dreamweaver/*
- *www.coffeecup.com*

- *https://diywebkit.com*

- *www.easy-business-websites.com*

- *www.easywebeditor.com*

- *www.freeserifsoftware.com/software/WebPlus/default.asp*

- *www.homestead.com*

- *www.ibuilt.net*

- *www.web.com*

- *www.webstudio.com*

Another very important issue in website design and management is Search-Engine Optimization (SEO), a complex topic related to how high you're listed in the search engines (e.g., Google, Internet Explorer, Netscape, Dogpile, Yahoo, AltaVista). For example, if you go to *www.google.com* and type in the word "resume," you'll get more than 427 million hits. And, as we all know, most people will search the websites that appear on the first few pages. Chances are they're never going to get to the business that's listed on page 129!

That's what SEO is all about—moving your business website to the top of the listings. It takes hard work, dedication, and a thorough understanding of how search engines rank websites in order to move your listing near the top. Although you may consider this a laborious task, it is an extremely important task in order to increase the traffic visiting your website.

One of my favorite resources for information on website design, website marketing, SEO, and scores of other related topics is SiteProNews (*www.sitepronews.com*). You can visit their website for detailed information and/or subscribe to their free email newsletter, both of which are excellent resources.

For additional information about the entire spectrum of website design and management, we recommend you visit these following websites for information, templates, and additional resources:

- *www.affinity.com*

- *www.allbusiness.com*

- *www.giantexplorer.com*

- *www.internet.com*

- *www.killersites.com*

- *www.knowledgestorm.com*
- *www.linxbest.com*
- *www.networksolutions.com*
- *www.networkworld.com*
- *www.seobook.com*
- *www.seotoday.com*
- *www.templatemonster.com*
- *www.useit.com*
- *www.web.com*
- *www.websitetips.com*

Blogs

If you pay a lot of attention to trends in website design, you'll already be familiar with blogs. Short for weblog, a blog is a specific type of website, where entries are made similar to a journal or diary, and then displayed in reverse-chronological order, from most recent to past. Most significantly, blogs have emerged as a relatively easy and cost-effective way to establish a Web presence without having to invest in the development and maintenance of a full-scale website.

Blogs often provide commentary or news on a particular subject (e.g., local politics, national politics, cuisine, travel, job search, publishing). Typically, blogs combine text, images, and links to other blogs, websites, and other media as they relate specifically to the topic under discussion. For more information on what blogging is and how to set up your own blog, visit these sites:

- *http://blogsearch.google.com/*
- *www.blogger.com*
- *www.blogsearchengine.com*
- *www.blogslisting.com*
- *www.blogstream.com*
- *www.blogwise.com*
- *www.ektron.com*

- *www.squarespace.com*
- *www.toadfire.com*
- *www.typepad.com*
- *www.wordpress.com*

Online Networking Tools

One of the newest technology applications to hit the market is online networking. Just as with the more traditional methods of networking, online networking has emerged as a great way to build and expand your network of contacts, share information and resources, build the visibility of your company, capture new customers, identify new business opportunities, and much more.

To capitalize on this growing phenomenon, online-networking communities have arisen. The most popular ones include:

Business Network International	*www.bni.com*
Ecademy.com	*www.ecademy.com*
Linked In	*www.linkedin.com*
Networking For Professionals	*www.networkingfor professionals.com*
Plaxo	*www.plaxo.com*
Ryze	*www.ryze.com*
Tribe	*http://washingtondc.tribe.net*

You can join these online-networking communities for free and have instant access to the thousands of other professionals who belong. However, just as with traditional networking, you need to work at it. It's not enough to simply join the community; rather, you must focus on building relationships with other members so that you can strengthen your online presence and your credibility. You can post information on topics in your area of expertise, respond to others' posts when you have relevant information to share, join sub-communities that focus on particular industries and/or professions, post resources on bulletin boards, and more. The more visible you are, the more you'll benefit from these relationships and, eventually, capture new business opportunities.

Here are a few important tips about online networking:

- **Position yourself as an expert.** Limit yourself to sharing information about which you truly are an expert (or, at least, have a strong wealth of knowledge). Don't over-post and destroy your credibility.

- **Strengthen your brand.** Every time you sign an email message or a posting, be sure to include your signature line (as discussed in the Email section earlier in this chapter). Your signature line should prominently display your brand (who you are/what your company does).

- **Start a buzz.** There is no better way to advertise than by word-of-mouth. If you have satisfied customers, they can market for your business by sharing their positive experiences.

- **Listen more than you talk.** Online networks can provide you with a wealth of information about your target markets and customers. Read carefully what others are writing about!

An important note of caution . . . don't join too many communities or you will not have the time that is necessary to effectively build and nurture your relationships. Choose just one or two, and then devote your time to building your visibility and credibility within those communities.

Protecting Yourself and Your Technology

Once you've invested the time and money in acquiring your computer hardware and software, installing your programs, inputting your data, and more, you want to be sure to protect all of that information. With viruses, worms, and spyware, it's a real jungle out there!

To better understand the potential threats to your technology, I'll start with definitions of the most common ones you may encounter:

- **Spam:** The electronic equivalent of junk mail, generally sent to a mailing list or newsgroup. More generally, spam is defined as unsolicited email. Note that there's really nothing dangerous about spam unless, of course, there is a virus or worm attached. It is simply an annoyance.

- **Spyware:** Software that transmits information about your Internet sessions back to the computer from which that information is sent to create marketing profiles based on surfing habits. Spyware is often built into free downloads and works in the background (as a spy) without a user's knowledge.

- **Virus:** A program that infects a computer by attaching itself to another program and propagating when that program is executed. Although some viruses are only pranks, others can destroy files, wipe out hard drives, and really make you "sick."

- **Worm:** A computer program that can make copies of itself, and spread through connected systems, using up resources in affected computers or causing other damage.

To protect yourself against these destructive programs, you'll definitely want to purchase:

- **Anti-Virus Program:** Software programs that detect, remove, and/or destroy viruses on your computer. Although these programs are not 100% effective since new viruses appear routinely, their track record is strong. For resources to learn more about and/or purchase anti-virus programs, visit these websites:

  - *www.anti-virus-software-review.toptenreviews.com*

  - *www.avast.com*

  - *www.checkpoint.com*

  - *www.earthlink.net/cybercheck*

  - *www.mcafee.com*

  - *www.microsoft.com/exchange*

  - *www.pandasoftware.com*

  - *http://us.trendmicro.com/us/home/home_user/index.html*

  - *www.pctools.com*

  - *www.stop-sign.com*

  - *www.symantec.com* (#1 anti-virus program, Norton Utilities)

- **Firewall:** Electronic boundary that prevents unauthorized users from accessing certain files on a network. For resources to learn more about and/or purchase firewalls, visit these websites:

- *http://firewalls.infoworld.com*
- *www.barracudanetworks.com*
- *www.firewallguide.com/software.htm*
- *www.microsoft.com/isaserver*
- *http://searchsecurity.techtarget.com*
- *www.zonealarm.com*

- **Spam Filter:** Program that detects unsolicited and unwanted email and prevents those messages from getting into a user's inbox. Like other types of filtering programs, a spam filter looks for certain criteria on which it bases judgments. For resources to learn more about and/or purchase anti-spam software, visit these websites:

  - *www.cloudmark.com*
  - *www.dedicatedserver.com*
  - *www.messagelabs.com*
  - *www.roaringpenguin.com*
  - *www.symantec.com*

Using Technology as Your Virtual Assistant

Virtual Assistant: *Individual or small business providing off-site secretarial, office-management, and administrative-support functions to individuals who do not need a full-time employee to handle those activities.*

Five years ago, most people had never heard of a Virtual Assistant (VA). Today, however, the VA industry is growing at a phenomenal rate as entrepreneurs, small-business owners, consultants, and other business professionals realize the tremendous value to be gained through such business relationships. In fact, if you do a search for "Virtual Assistant" on *www.google.com*, you'll find that there are 48 million hits!

One of the greatest benefits to working with a Virtual Assistant is the cost savings that you'll enjoy. Since VAs are self-employed, you are not responsible for withholding taxes, paying matching Social Security (FICA) taxes, providing benefits, or any one of the many other financial obligations you have when you hire an employee. What's more, since they are self-employed and, we would assume, motivated to generate income, VAs will generally offer you excellent service, loyalty, flexibility, and reliability, all characteristics that you would desire in any employee or temporary worker.

Virtual Assistants can perform a diversity of business-support functions for you and your business:

- New business start-up and office set-up
- Secretarial and word-processing projects
- Correspondence management
- Documents and records management
- Answering service
- Travel and meeting planning
- Project management
- Writing and editing
- Newsletters and press releases
- Research
- Scheduling
- Bookkeeping
- Website management
- Email management
- Marketing and sales support
- Personal assistance

In fact, you can most likely find a Virtual Assistant who is willing to do just about anything that you need, within reason, to support your business operations. Typically, VAs charge between $20 and $50 per hour. However, those with more specialized experience (e.g., legal, medical, scientific), may charge as much as $100 or more per hour. Most VAs do work on an hourly basis, although some, much like consultants, prefer to have retainer agreements with their clients who commit to paying for 10, 20, or more hours each month.

To research the VA industry or to locate a virtual assistant to help with your business needs, we recommend these following resources:

- International Association of
  Virtual Office Assistants   *www.iavoa.com*

- International Virtual
  Assistant Association   *www.ivaa.org*

- Virtual Business Group   *www.virtualbizgroup.com*

Great Technology Resources

Following is a list of some popular books on technology, most of which were written for non-technologists like myself. As such, they're easy to read, understand, and apply to your specific needs and business situation.

- *Beyond Bullet Points: Using Microsoft PowerPoint to Create Presentations that Inform, Motivate, and Inspire* (Cliff Atkinson)

- *Computer Telephone: Automating Home Offices and Small Businesses* (Ed Tittel and Dawn Rader)

- *Creating Web Pages for Dummies* (Bud E. Smith and Arthur Bebak)

- *Don't Make Me Think: A Common-Sense Approach to Web Usability* (Steve Krug)

- *Guerilla Marketing with Technology: Unleashing the Full Potential of Your Small Business* (Jay Conrad Levinson)

- *Learning Web Design* (Jennifer Niederst)

- *Managing Information Technology in Small Business: Challenges and Solutions* (Stephen Burgess)

- *Net Words: Creating High-Impact Online Copy* (Nick Usbourne)

- *Small Business Guide to Computers & Office Automation: A Comprehensive Overview of Computers and Modern Office Technology, and How to Select a System* (Neil E. Perlin)

- *Starting an eBay Business for Dummies* (Marsha Collier)

- *The Design of Sites* (Douglas K. van Duyne)

- *The Home Office and Small Business Answer Book* (Janet Attard)

- *The Official eBay Guide to Buying, Selling and Collecting Just About Anything* (Laura Fisher Kaiser and Michael B. Kaiser)

- *The SEO Book* (Aaron Wall)

- *The Unofficial Guide to Starting a Small Business* (Marcia Layton Turner)

There are hundreds of thousands of online resources that you can explore. To help you get started, here are a few of the most popular for developing your suite of technology tools:

Apple Computers	*www.apple.com/business*
Business Technology Association	*www.bta.org*
Business Week	*www.businessweek.com*
Business.com	*www.business.com/directory/ management/software/*
CNN	*www.cnn.com/tech*
Forbes	*www.forbes.com/technology/*
Glossarist	*www.glossarist.com/glossaries/ technology*
High-Tech Dictionary	*www.computeruser.com/ resources/dictionary/ dictionary.html*
Information Week	*www.informationweek.com*
Microsoft	*www.microsoft.com*
News.com	*http://news.com.com/?tag= ne.tab.hd*
Small Business Administration	*www.sba.gov/SBIR/*
Small Business Technology Institute	*www.sbtechnologyinstitute.org/*
SmallBizTechnology	*www.smallbiztechnology.com*
TechConfidential	*www.techconfidential.com*
Tech Dictionary	*www.techdictionary.com*

- **TechEncyclopedia**   *www.techweb.com/*
                                  encyclopedia

- **Technology Dictionary**   *www.techdict.org*

- **Webopedia**   *www.webopedia.com*

- **Whatis.com**   *http://whatis.techtarget.com*

9 How Well Do You Juggle?
Managing Your Time and Productivity

I F YOU HAVE A TRUE entrepreneurial spirit and an inner drive to succeed, you'll find that you're constantly trying to identify ways to:

- Do things faster
- Do things more efficiently
- Do things better
- Get more things done every day
- Maximize your productivity
- Leverage your skills to expand your capabilities
- Excel at everything that you do

And that is precisely what this chapter is about—how to increase your productivity and efficiency, improve your performance, optimize the use of your time, find more time in each day, eliminate time wasters, and juggle everything that the typical entrepreneur must manage. I've included lots of helpful hints, strategies, tools, and resources in this chapter that have been designed specifically to improve your time-management capabilities and help you identify ways to increase your own personal productivity and efficiency.

One very important note before I proceed . . . people tend to be most productive when they're doing what they're good at, what they enjoy, and what they believe to be valuable. This is a critically important concept as you begin to develop and build your business. In the long run, if you're doing something that comes easily to you, in which you have a wealth of knowledge and competency, and which fulfills you, you will find that your entrepreneurial venture is a much more positive, personally satisfying, and financially rewarding career path.

Productivity and peak performance arise from your own personal capabilities, competencies, and commitment. Be certain that you've selected a business venture that taps into all three of those core entrepreneurial-success factors.

Time-Management Tools

Time management is really all about making 48 hours out of 24! What can you do to optimize the use of your time, get more done each day, and eliminate those tasks that interrupt your workday and interfere with your schedule? Here are a few recommendations that have proven to be extremely effective in allowing entrepreneurs to better control their time and, in turn, improve their personal productivity and business output.

5 D's of Pile Management

If you're like most entrepreneurs, you may often find yourself surrounded by piles and piles of papers, notes, projects, files, bills, books, mail, client materials, product literature, tech manuals, and so much more. In fact, there may be times when you wonder where it all came from, what to do with it, or how to get rid of it. Here's a system for effectively managing your piles, reducing your piles, and eliminating your piles so that you don't get buried beneath it all.

- **Do It.** Sometimes, the most efficient behavior is to do something with each thing the moment that you receive it. Don't lay it on your desk or pile it on your floor to take care of later. This may be as easy as filing away a bank statement as soon as you receive it in the mail, or unpacking a shipment of books and shelving them immediately upon receipt. Don't create more piles and work for yourself than you need to. Simply do it now and be done with it!

- **Determine When to Do It.** Inevitably, there will be things that simply can't be done at the exact moment in time that you receive them. However, they still need to be taken care of. My best recommendation is to determine when to do them and then schedule them into your calendar so they're out of sight and out of mind until such time that you need to address them. If you keep everything piled on or near your desk, important items may end up being buried under other materials, or you may simply forget about them. If they're scheduled to be taken care of at a later date, you're off the hook, can devote your time to what needs to be done today, and be confident that they won't get overlooked.

- **Delegate It.** As your business grows, many entrepreneurs find that they simply cannot get everything done themselves. This will be the point in time when you make the determination to hire staff, contractors, temporary workers, consultants, or advisors. And one of the greatest benefits of adding personnel to your team is being able to delegate certain tasks to them. Many small-business entrepreneurs often find that the first people they hire are those who can do the tasks they dread the most and/or are the least competent doing. For me, one of the first people I added to my team was an individual who could manage my bookkeeping and accounting functions, tasks that I don't enjoy or am not particularly good at doing. Remember, I'm a writer and a trainer!

- **Dungeon It.** Simply put, to dungeon something means to file it away. There will, of course, be materials that you'll want to keep, but which you do not need at hand each and every single day. As such, file these materials away so that you can access them when necessary, but get them off your desk, off the floor, and out of sight.

- **Destroy It.** There are certain things that you simply do not need to keep. You're never going to use them, read them, refer to them, or have any other use for them, so get rid of them. This normally means one of three things: either you'll throw the materials away, put them in a box for recycling, or shred them to protect confidentiality. For those of you who tend to keep everything, you'll need to find a way to force yourself to eliminate some your piles or you may find that you can never come up for air.

Touch It Only Once

Another strategy that goes hand-in-hand with effective pile management is the concept of touching things only once. One of the greatest traps you can fall into is touching things, moving them, moving them again, re-piling them, and shuffling them from one spot to another on your desk. In the end, you'll find that you're lost behind the piles of everything that you've amassed and are spending more time reorganizing and rearranging materials than doing productive work.

To ensure that this doesn't happen to you, attempt to only touch things once. As you have them in your hand for the very first time, do something with them rather than just setting them down. Here are a few great examples:

- One of your suppliers has just faxed you a two-page contract for the purchase of electronic components essential for the product that you manufacture. Assuming you're familiar with this supplier and have ordered from them in the past, review the faxed contract as soon as you receive it, sign it, and fax it back. In just a few minutes you're finished, rather than piling it somewhere to take care of in the future.   *Do it!*

- A client has promised to send you back-up information for a project that you have scheduled to work on in two weeks. When that material arrives, simply put it into your calendar for the date that you have it scheduled. Then, it's out of sight and off your desk until such time that you actually need to work on it.   *Determine When!*

- Almost each day, you receive invoices, payments, bank statements, credit-card statements, and other financial materials. Fortunately, you now have a part-time book-keeper who is responsible for managing those items. As such, as soon as they arrive, put them immediately into an inbox for your bookkeeper and never look at them again.
                                Delegate it!

- Over the next year, you plan to upgrade your telecommunications system. As such, you've been collecting (and piling) information about various telecommunications companies, services, and options, knowing that you won't make a final decision for months to come. Rather than keeping all of this material piled on a desk or table for the next year, file it away for easy reference when you're ready to make your purchasing decision.   ***Dungeon it!***

- You pick up the daily mail and immediately realize that more than half are advertisements and credit-card promotions. As you touch each one of these items, simply throw them into your recycling bin and you're done with them.   ***Destroy it!***

If you're able to implement these time-management tools to optimize what you do and when you do it, you'll find that you're more productive and more efficient in the operation and management of your entrepreneurial venture.

Eliminating Time Wasters

If you sit back and look closely at the things that you waste your time doing, you'll find that they generally fall into one of two categories:

- Internal Time Wasters
- External Time Wasters

Internal time wasters are those items and activities that come from within. This includes things such as shuffling and rearranging the piles on your desk 20 times a day, to re-tracing the activities that your purchasing agent performed to ensure that he/she did their job well. To control the internal time wasters that can easily gobble up your time each and every day, I recommend these specific action items:

1. **If you've hired someone to do a job, and you're confident that you made a good hiring decision, *let that person do their job!*** Don't feel obliged to follow them around to be sure that everything is being handled in the exact same manner in which you would manage it. If you devoted the time necessary to train an individual on a particular function, then feel some level of confidence in the fact that they know what they're

doing. If you feel the need to check each and every thing that they've done, you might as well just do it yourself!

2. **Jumping from one project to another can use up your time in no time at all!** If you find that you are constantly moving from one activity to another—and not completing anything—you'll want to consider restructuring how you manage your day and your responsibilities. Refer to the "Chunking or Project Completion" section later in this chapter to better understand about the two different options for task management and completion.

3. **Devote time each day to managing the piles on your desk.** This will be discussed in greater length in the section of this chapter, "Productivity and Efficiency Management Tools." However, suffice it to say that you can find yourself wasting a tremendous amount of time each and every day if you continually feel the need to review the materials on your desk, rearrange them, put them into other piles, and more. This is where the 5 D's of Pile Management really come into play.

4. **Reading the newspaper, watering the plants in your office, calling to speak to friends . . .** the list of potential internal time wasters goes on and on. The fact of the matter is that you'll most likely engage in these activities when you're trying to avoid what really needs to be done. If you find that you're having difficulty focusing on the business task at hand—and you don't want to fritter away the day—consider working on a simpler task first. Once that's complete, you most likely will find that you're back on track and ready to tackle the less-than-desirable project or activity that really needs your attention.

On the other side of the spectrum are external time wasters, those items and activities which are externally driven. Examples include email, personal phone calls, unannounced visits, and more. To control the external items that interrupt your time each day, consider these specific action items:

1. **Explain to your family and friends that, during the workday, you're tied up with clients, projects, and work-related functions.** As such, ask them to please save their phone calls and visits until after work hours so that you can optimize the use of your time when you're on the job.

2. **Turn the sound off on your email** so that each and every time you receive a new email message, you're not interrupted. I'm not advocating that you ignore your email; rather, I'm recommending that you check it on a regular basis (e.g., every hour or two, twice in the morning and twice in the afternoon) rather than checking each individual message as it's received.

3. **Certain phone calls will require your immediate attention and, therefore, are considered high-priority items.** However, many other calls will not be critical and, therefore, should not be allowed to interrupt your daily workflow. If, for example, you're in the middle of an important, deadline-driven task, let your voice mail answer the call or have someone else in your office pick up the phone. This will allow you to complete the project at hand and then take the time later to return calls as necessary.

4. **Close your office door** when you need to and tell your staff not to interrupt you unless it's extremely important. One of the greatest plagues that beset business owners is the constant interruptions to their workday. Some of these interruptions (e.g., your production line has closed down) are critical and do require your immediate attention. Others, however, such as a question about a credit memo, are not critical. Therefore, if you're working on something important, nicely communicate to your staff that you'd like some uninterrupted work time to complete the task at hand.

Time-Management Model

The chart on the next page provides you with a graphic representation for how to best optimize your time to ensure that the most critical and most time-sensitive materials are taken care of immediately, while the less important items are put on the back burner until you have time to address them. Use this chart as a guide to help you determine which items are high-priority and which are not.

Productivity and Efficiency-Improvement Tools

How can you be more productive and more efficient? This is a question that all entrepreneurs and businesspersons ask themselves over and over.

Time-Management Model

	Time-Sensitive	Not Time-Sensitive
Important	Crises and Emergencies	Business Planning
	Deadline-Driven Projects	Relationship Building
	Activities with Due Dates	Preventative Maintenance
	Customer Inquiries	Exploring Opportunities
	Customer Follow-Up	Hiring Personnel
	Paying Bills	Reviewing Business Plan

	Time-Sensitive	Not Time-Sensitive
Not Important	Some Mail and Email	Some Mail and Email
	Some Phone Calls	Some Phone Calls
	Some Meetings	Busy Work

What can they do to accomplish more each day, believing that the more productive they are, the more successful their business venture will be, and the more money they will make? And the reality is that productivity does impact performance and profitability.

To ensure that you're optimizing your productivity and working as efficiently as possible, consider these important items and how they can positively impact your daily performance.

"Chunking" or Project Completion

No matter what type of business you launch or the specific products or services that you provide, there are really only two distinct models for personal-productivity management—"chunking" and project completion. It is important to note that I'm talking about personal productivity and not the productivity of your specific business (e.g., manufacturing yield, sales-call volume, service volume, annual revenue run).

Many people find that they are most effective when they work in defined segments of time . . . chunks. For example, it may be that you know you're most productive in 35-minute intervals. After that, you begin to get itchy and feel the need to get up out of your chair, engage in a different activity, check on the status of others at work, or something else.

On the other hand, people who operate via the project-completion method find their greatest rewards from completing a particular project, assignment, or work activity. If you operate via this method, you may find that you often work very long hours in order to finish the task at hand, knowing that when it's completed, you will feel a great sense of satisfaction.

Neither method is better than the other. The difference lies in which motivates and propels you to be most productive and most efficient. If you're uncertain as to which is your particular style, test each one of them out and you'll quickly be able to determine which gives you the most satisfaction. Being productive has one more great benefit ... it makes you even more motivated and more productive!

Chained to Your Desk

Believe it or not, the effective administration of your business will definitely contribute to your bottom-line profitability. However, many entrepreneurs are much more interested in producing and delivering their products and services than they are in managing the paperwork required to support the business. Consider the landscaping contractor who spends the vast majority of his time selling and then completing landscape projects. He may see little value in spending time sitting at a desk when the real money is made out in the field.

Be forewarned, however, that this can be a critical mistake! Managing your business is as important as operating your business. If you don't manage well and if you don't attend to the countless administrative details of business ownership, you may find that you won't have a business at all in years to come.

I recommend that you spend a minimum of at least 15 minutes each day at your desk to organize your day, your resources, your materials, your staff, and, most importantly, your brain. Some entrepreneurs do this first thing in the morning each day in preparation for that day's work; others prefer to do it at the end of each day in preparation for tomorrow's work. Either way, it's an essential component of your business success.

Obviously, there are also other times that you'll need to spend at your desk, no matter your particular type of business venture. Certain things will always need to be taken care of—bills paid, phone calls returned, job interviews conducted, and so much more. However, that 15 minutes of time that you devote each day to organizing your work life is invaluable in controlling and effectively managing your business operations.

Prioritize for Efficiency

Consider this scenario. You're surrounded by piles of projects, phone calls to return, lists of materials that need to be purchased, and more, all of which are important to complete within the week. However, you only have 30 minutes left before you need to leave your office for the day. What can you do in that 30 minutes that, hopefully, you can start and finish in such a limited amount of time?

This is what's known as prioritizing for efficiency. In essence, it's quickly evaluating what needs to be done and what you can do in the time that you have available. Rather than starting a major project that may take hours or days to complete, when you only have a few minutes, select an item or two that you can easily, quickly, and efficiently complete in the allocated time. If you do this, you'll be amazed at how productive you can be and how quickly the piles on your desk disappear.

All too many start-up entrepreneurs forget one of the most important factors in effective prioritization—do your hard work when you're fresh and save the easy stuff for when you're tired. Makes sense, doesn't it? Do your hard work—the difficult projects, complex technical programming, contract negotiations, and more—when you're fresh, alert, and ready to tackle the day. Conversely, save the easy stuff—phone calls, filing, bill paying, stock replenishment, housekeeping chores, and more—for the end of the day, when you're tired and have just a few minutes to spare.

Automate Key Business Functions

The reality is that certain business functions—bookkeeping, credit-card processing, written communications, and more—are most efficiently managed when you use the appropriate technology tools. The days of manually computing customer invoices, manually recording inventory volumes, and manually tracking shipments are long gone. Thank heavens!

In order to ensure your optimum productivity, be certain that you take the time that is necessary to identify and implement the right technologies to expedite and streamline your business functions. Refer to Chapter 8, *Technology: It's a Tool, Not a Solution*, for detailed information on the different technology and telecommunications tools you may need to integrate into your business to meet your operating needs.

When All Else Fails ...

When all else fails, let deadlines force you to produce! By no means is this the best strategy to optimize your productivity and efficiency. However, it does work. I know from experience! What's more, as a start-up entrepreneur, you may often find yourself working to meet constant deadlines and obligations. Inevitably, you'll be faced with this situation, so use it to your advantage.

One of the surprising things about working under pressure is that you often produce your very best work. You would assume the opposite would be true, and it can be, but from my experience I can honestly tell you that working under the gun can produce outstanding results. I believe it's a result of trusting your own instincts and not over-thinking each and every thing. If you don't have time to waste, you decide what to do, how to do it, and you simply do it. A common characteristic of many successful entrepreneurs is that they have great gut instincts and intuition. Learn to trust yours!

One very important note of caution: Even when deadlines force you to produce, there is no excuse for not meeting those deadlines. Being late—on client projects, customer services, product sales, tax returns, and more—is simply not acceptable (barring true emergencies)!

If It Works for You, It's Okay

There's a great old book that, unfortunately, is now out of print although you can probably find a copy at a used bookstore. *Shenson on Consulting* was written by a famed management consultant, Howard L. Shenson, and includes excellent information on a diversity of consulting, customer-relationship management, pricing, productivity, and time-management issues. At the very end of the book, Shenson talks about entrepreneurs, consultants, and their often-unique working schedules and hours. He comments that although your friends, family, and colleagues may think that you're crazy, if it works for you, it's okay.

For some of us, the very early morning is the most productive, while others find that evenings and nights are more productive.

This concept extends beyond just scheduling to include all facets of owning and operating your own business. It includes the systems that you develop, the processes, procedures, policies, operating functions, and more. The point is to develop business operations and practices that work for you, for your company, and for your customers. Bottom-line, that's all that matters.

Lists and Index Cards

I simply love lists. I like writing them because it gives me a plan of action for what needs to be done that day, what needs to be done for a particular customer or project, what things I need to take care of over the next week, what supplies I need to order, whom I need to call, and so much more. However, what I really enjoy about lists is crossing items off of them! There is something very rewarding about the physicality of actually drawing a thick line through an item or putting a big checkmark next to it. Done! What a great feeling it is to actually see that I'm being productive.

I'll even let you in on a little secret! If I find that I've done something that isn't on my list, I'll add it to the list just so I can get the satisfaction of crossing it off. Odd, I know, but I really do get tremendous joy and a sense of completion out of doing it.

I also adore 3 x 5 index cards, not 4 x 6. I particularly like them in yellow and red, and use them for all kinds of different things. When I'm first starting to think about my next book project, I prepare a chapter outline (on one index card) and then devote one index card to each chapter to keep track of my ideas. I use them all the time when I'm teaching workshops and seminars, and find them particularly effective for keeping track of certain project components.

Many people may think that my paper systems are antiquated, but, frankly, they work the best for me. As you read in Chapter 8, *Technology: It's a Tool, Not a Solution*, not everything has to be computerized, automated, and technologically driven in order to be efficient. In fact, as you can see, some of my very best time and productivity systems are based on good, old-fashioned paper-and-pencil tools.

On the next few pages are some of my favorite list and task management forms. Feel free to customize them to fit your specific needs. All of these forms can be easily computerized if technology tools work best for you.

DAILY TASK MANAGEMENT*

Date: _____

Must Do:
(Deadline-driven, critical)

1. _____
2. _____
3. _____
4. _____
5. _____
6. _____

Should Do:
(Important)

1. _____
2. _____
3. _____
4. _____
5. _____
6. _____

If Time Permits:
(Low-priority, yet essential)

1. _____
2. _____
3. _____
4. _____
5. _____
6. _____

* Prepare your **Daily Task Management** worksheet on a day-by-day basis as your priorities and obligations change, new critical items come to the forefront, and other items become less important.

WEEKLY TASK MANAGEMENT*

Week: _____

Must Do:
(Deadline-
driven, critical)

1. _____
2. _____
3. _____
4. _____
5. _____
6. _____

Should Do:
(Important)

1. _____
2. _____
3. _____
4. _____
5. _____
6. _____

If Time
Permits:
(Low-priority,
yet essential)

1. _____
2. _____
3. _____
4. _____
5. _____
6. _____

* Prepare 4 **Weekly Task Management** worksheets at a time—on a month-by-month basis—to keep track of items that are important, but don't necessarily need to be taken care of that day.

MONTHLY TASK MANAGEMENT*

Month: _____

Must Do:
(Deadline-driven, critical)

1. _____

2. _____

3. _____

4. _____

5. _____

6. _____

Should Do:
(Important)

1. _____

2. _____

3. _____

4. _____

5. _____

6. _____

If Time Permits:
(Low-priority, yet essential)

1. _____

2. _____

3. _____

4. _____

5. _____

6. _____

* Prepare 12 **Monthly Task Management** worksheets—one for each month—so that you can quickly jot down any upcoming projects, activities, business, housekeeping functions, and more.

Great Resources for Organization, Time Management and Productivity Improvement

Books

- *Conquering Chronic Disorganization*   Judith Kohlberg
- *Eat That Frog! 21 Great Ways to Stop Procrastinating*   Brian Tracy
- *Focal Point: A Proven System to Simplify Your Life*   Brian Tracy
- *Get Your Act Together!*   Pam Young
- *Getting Things Done*   David Allen
- *Goal Setting 101*   Gary Ryan Blair
- *Make Success Measurable: A Mindbook-Workbook*   Douglas K. Smith
- *Motivation and Goal Setting*   Jim Cairo
- *Organizing From the Inside Out*   Julie Morgenstern
- *Take Time for Your Life*   Cheryl Richardson
- *The 7 Habits of Highly Effective People*   Stephen R. Covey
- *The 80 / 20 Individual*   Richard Koch
- *The 80 / 20 Principle*   Richard Koch
- *The Idiot's Guide to Time Management*   Jeff Davidson
- *The Procrastinator's Handbook*   Rita Emmett
- *The Tactics of Very Successful People*   B. Eugene Griessman
- *Time Management From the Inside Out*   Julie Morgenstern

Websites

- *http://BottomLineSecrets.com*   Bottom Line Personal newsletter
- *www.balancetime.com*   Dr. Don Wetmore's time-management seminars
- *www.flylady.com*   Household organization strategies

- *www.jugglezine.com*   Dedicated to finding
                                 balance in work and life

- *www.manage-your-time.com*   Articles and reviews
                                 on products

- *www.mindtools.com*   Reviews and links to
                                 resources

- *www.onlineorganizing.com*   Organizing products
                                 and services

10 Soaring High:
Secrets to Long-Term Entrepreneurial Success

MOST OF THIS BOOK HAS FOCUSED on starting a new entrepreneurial venture—what you need to do, why, how, and when. Now, let's switch gears and focus on all of the things you need to do in order to ensure the long-term operational and financial success of your business.

Owning a business is no easy job! And, if you're under the illusion that once you've launched your business, things will get easier, then you're way off base. Things will change, of course, but the reality is that entrepreneurship will never get easier. It will just become different. You'll get smarter, learn lots of new things, significantly expand your skill set, do things you never thought possible, and, hopefully, make a lot of money.

Being an entrepreneur—one whose business thrives—requires a unique blend of professional skills and competencies. Most significantly, owning your own business requires:

- A tremendous amount of work—today, tomorrow, and forever.

- An intense inner drive and motivation to succeed.

- The ability to make tough decisions and stick by them.

- The guts to stand strong when you need to.

- The mindset that you can live comfortably with the risk.

- The ability to communicate well—with your customers, employees, vendors, partners, and others.

- An obsessive commitment to quality—of your products, services, solutions, customer relationships, and business operations.

- A solid understanding of your money—revenues, expenses, budgets, projections, income statements, savings plans, and more.

- A strong and steadfast business infrastructure that effectively supports your operation.

- An unflappable commitment to building and operating your very best business.

One of the most important lessons that all entrepreneurs learn over time is that it's really not all about money. Although the money is extremely important, in the end, you want to be able to look back and take pride in the business that you built and how well it performed. You'll want to leave a legacy of success behind you as you move on to the post-entrepreneurial phase of your life.

This chapter reveals insider secrets for long-term entrepreneurial success—success that can be measured in terms of profits, income, customer satisfaction, quality, and personal fulfillment. It also addresses some of the common lifestyle issues that plague many entrepreneurs—figuring out how to manage the constant demands of their business while still having a life. It really is a tremendous challenge.

Next, I'll discuss the concepts of business growth, expansion, and diversification—issues that will become critical the longer you've been in business. Another section talks about entrepreneurial elegance—etiquette and protocol—for the successful entrepreneur. And, finally, I'll explore what may happen when you reach the end of your entrepreneurial path.

Chart Your Progress

No matter who you are or what type of business you own, there will be days when you question everything that you're doing and working towards, and wonder if it might just be easier to get a job. These days happen to the best of us, no matter what we do or how many years we've been in business. It's an inevitable part of the entrepreneurial lifecycle and you're going to have to learn to live with it.

To help you get over those hurdles and revitalize yourself, you should prepare the following. These items will prove invaluable on those sullen days when you are questioning your choices and your life.

1. **Buy a beautifully designed notebook** (or use your computer if you prefer) to keep track of each and every one of your achievements. This is going to be a running timeline of your entrepreneurial success and a valuable reference tool as time marches on. What you include in this notebook will vary from one entrepreneur to the other, depending entirely on the specific type of business that you own. Successes may include such things as:

   - Revenue and profit performance
   - Major projects and achievements
   - Key clients/customers
   - Increases in market-share ratings
   - Major cost-savings and cost-avoidance programs
   - New product innovations
   - New service offerings
   - Publications (e.g., articles, newsletters, books)
   - Trademarks and patents
   - Technological advances

2. **Keep a file of all testimonials**, thank-you letters, acknowledgments, letters of reference, letters of recommendation, and the like that you receive from satisfied clients and colleagues.

3. **Keep a file of all professional honors** and awards that you receive.

4. **Keep a file of all the media coverage** that you and/or your business receives, whether it's a brief one-line mention of your company or a full-page article.

These materials are also a wonderful addition to your marketing communications portfolio (e.g., sales literature, advertisements, promotions, product literature) that we discussed in Chapter 4, *Building Your Empire*.

Testimonials, professional honors and distinctions, publications, and more instantly communicate a message of credibility, professionalism, and quality to prospective customers, and can be instrumental in helping you to penetrate new markets and close new sales.

Problem Solving Made Easy

Solving problems—big ones and little ones—is a routine part of every entrepreneur's responsibilities. Situations will arise that you never anticipated, and you need to be well equipped to deal with them as expediently and effectively as possible. In fact, all too many entrepreneurs are under the impression that once they've struggled through the start-up phases of their businesses and established themselves as profitable companies, all of their problems will magically disappear. If it were only that easy!

Every business faces challenges—today, tomorrow, and in the future. The problems will be different in the start-up phases versus the ongoing operation of your business, but they will exist nonetheless. What will set you apart and propel you to success is your ability to deal with, address, and resolve those problems.

Double-guessing the decisions that you've made and the entrepreneurial course that you've launched are not the answer. Those choices have already been made. You can, of course, alter your course as need be, but there's no point in looking back and wondering about "what if?" scenarios. That action will get you nowhere.

To help you approach your business challenges with a clear mind and decisive path, I've created a five-step action plan that can be used to address, investigate, and resolve virtually any problem you may encounter in your business. This can include problems with financial affairs, marketing, sales, customer relations, manufacturing, product performance, service delivery, purchasing, logistics, technology, telecommunications, and so forth. It is important to note that the more detailed you are with your responses to the following questions, the more effective your final plan will be.

Step 1.
Define the specific problem.

- What is the specific problem?

- How did this problem arise?

- What, if anything, am I currently doing about the problem?

- What other aspects and functions within my business is this problem impacting?
- If I've tried to resolve the problem in the past, did my strategy or action work?
- How much is this problem costing me?

Step 2.
Who can help me with this problem?

- Do I have employees or other personnel who may be able to help me solve this problem?
- Can my Board of Directors or Board of Advisors help solve this problem?
- Do I have professional colleagues who might be willing to help me with this problem?
- Should I consult my attorney, my accountant, or another business professional?
- Can my family or friends be of any help in addressing this issue?

Step 3.
Consider all the possibilities for solving the problem.

- What are all of the different things that I could do to solve this problem?
- What would my competition do if they were faced with a similar problem?
- What have others done in the past to solve such problems?
- Is there a way of seeing this problem as a potential opportunity to improve my business or better serve my customers?

Step 4.
Evaluate the reasonableness of each possibility.

- Which of the possibilities I listed is the most reasonable and why?

- What obstacles may stand in my way?

- What resources, personnel, materials, and/or equipment will I need to take the recommended action?

- How long will it take to implement this solution?

- Are there any potentially negative outcomes to this solution?

- Am I confident in my ability to implement this solution?

Step 5.
Make a decision as to your specific course of action.

- What are the specific action steps I'll need to take in order to implement this solution?

- What can I do to ensure that this solution is successful?

- Can my staff or anyone else help with implementation?

- What are the long-term projected benefits of this solution?

The first few times you use this model, you may question its true validity and value to you. However, rest assured, that a step-by-step approach to resolving any business problem is the most reasonable and effective method to eliminate your roadblocks to success.

The Entrepreneurial Lifestyle

The entrepreneurial lifestyle is unique and generally revolves almost entirely around your business—whether you're in the office, at the factory, or lying in bed at home. Millions of thoughts, ideas, problems, and issues will constantly be running through your head:

- What projects are due when?

- What clients do you have to see?

- Have I scheduled an appointment with my attorney to review that new contract?

- What products must be manufactured and shipped? What tax returns are due?

- Who's going to take Gloria's place in the Accounting Department?

- What happened to the electronics order I placed two weeks ago?
- How much is it going to cost to repair the forklift?

As your business grows and you hire additional personnel, you probably think that your workload will lighten, but that's generally not the case. It may be that your responsibilities shift from doing a task to managing people who do a task, or that you spend a great of your time developing new products, creating new services, exploring new market opportunities, and so much more. The lifestyle of an entrepreneur is a huge commitment—one that will follow you no matter where you are or what you're doing. In essence, you're always on!

In this section, I'll share key lessons that I've learned about effectively managing my own entrepreneurial self and lifestyle. I'll address some of the common challenges that plague most entrepreneurs, share a few of my favorite entrepreneurial strategies, and demonstrate how to optimize your life—to meet your personal and professional goals.

Entrepreneurial Cycles

Every entrepreneur will pass through certain stages in their professional life. It's a natural occurrence as you pass through various stages in your own personal life—chronological stages, emotional stages, spiritual stages, and more. What inspired you to launch your business venture will invariably change over time, and what motivates you today is not necessarily what will motivate you next year. Change is an inevitable process, so expect it and embrace it, for it is the status quo.

Change drives us to think and act. If everything and everyone stayed the status quo, just think how boring and routine our lives would be. Rather, it's change that keeps us moving forward, trying new things, experimenting with new ideas, and striving to reach new pinnacles. It's change that has led to great inventions, great discoveries, and remarkable shifts in our economy.

Know that you and your business will be impacted by life changes and strive to optimize the results of those changes. As you begin to see a shift in what you value and consider important, pay close attention to how your business can best respond to those same changes. Always remember that your business is organic and transitions as does every other living thing.

One is the Loneliest Number

If you're a solo entrepreneur, you must be very careful not to isolate yourself from the rest of the world. This is particularly true if your business is home-based, you have no employees, and you have little direct interaction with your customers.

No one can operate in total isolation. And since work often provides us with our communities, you're going to have to find alternative ways to build your own community. For some people, this may not be an issue at all. They have loads of friends, are active in various community organizations, and already have an existing professional community of colleagues.

For others, however, this can be more difficult, and you may find yourself feeling cut off from the world. To avoid that, I recommend that you get out—join your local Chamber of Commerce, join your industry's professional association, attend conferences and seminars, join a networking group, or any one of a number of other venues that will allow you to be part of something that is bigger than just your business.

Get a Coach

Athletes have always known how important a coach is to their success. However, it's only been in the past 10 years that business coaching has emerged as a profession in its own right, and entrepreneurs have learned what valuable contributions coaches can make to their success.

What can a business coach do for you? A coach will help you define your purpose, determine the right direction for your business, identify problems, eliminate obstacles, evaluate new ideas, and, most importantly, make you accountable. If you've told your coach that you'll have a list of product alternatives ready to share by next week, you'd better be prepared. Coaches can be tough. It's their job to push you forward and help you meet the constantly changing challenges of business ownership and self-employment.

Whether you're in the start-up stages of launching your entrepreneurial venture, own a well-established company, or are plagued with operating problems, a coach can make a real difference in your short-range and long-term success. I strongly recommend you consider hiring one to help you and your business move forward. To find a qualified business coach, visit these resources:

- **Career Masters Institute**   *www.cminstitute.com*
- **Career Coach Academy**   *www.careercoachacademy.com*

- **Career Coach Institute**   *www.careercoachinstitute.com*
- **Coach Connection**   *www.findyourcoach.com*
- **Coach U**   *www.coachinc.com*
- **Entrepreneur.com**   *www.entrepreneur.com*
- **International Coach Federation**   *www.coachfederation.org*
- **Small Business Administration**   *www.sbanetwork.org*
- **World Assn. of Business Coaches**   *www.wabccoaches.com*

If you're serious about retaining a business coach, here are my recommendations for identifying the right coach for you and your business:

- **Find a business coach who has at least several years of experience in coaching.** Since this is a relatively new profession, you'll find that thousands of individuals are entering the coaching industry each year. Be sure to do your research to find a well-qualified individual.

- **Select a business coach who has some experience in the particular industry or profession in which you are engaged.** Although this is not a mandatory prerequisite, it certainly can be an added bonus. Coaches who understand your business, your products, your services, and your markets can often provide you with more decisive direction and guidance.

- **Don't worry about the geographic location of the coach that you select.** It is not necessary that you work face-to-face with your coach. In fact, more and more coaches are now working via phone and email with their clients, and the process works efficiently and remarkably well.

- **Don't engage a business coach who wants you to commit to a long-term contract or agreement.** In order to ensure that a particular coach is indeed the *right* coach for you will take a few sessions. Then, if at that time, you determine that you're not making the progress that you intended, it might be time to change coaches and find someone who will be more compatible with, and responsive to, your specific needs (assuming that your expectations are realistic).

- **Be realistic when working with a coach.** Coaches do not provide you with the answers. Rather, they ask you the *right* questions and encourage the *right* actions so that you can come to your own conclusions. Coaches are not "yes men." Rather, they will coach you to reach your own decisions and your own best performance.

Open Your Ears

Savvy entrepreneurs know that they can never get enough feedback, insight, or recommendations. They realize that they don't know everything and, therefore, are constantly on a learning curve, striving to increase their knowledge, expand their skills, fine-tune their capabilities, and so much more. As part of that process, they've learned to open themselves up to everyone, get as much advice as they possibly can, learn from it all, and then, most importantly, rely on their gut instincts and make their own decisions.

The fact is that no one is ever going to know your business as well as you do or be as committed to your success. Although you are always going to be searching for new information, new ways to do things better, new products and services to launch, and new ideas to explore, ultimately, you have to be the final decision maker. If you're already established and doing well in your business, trust that your gut instincts must be pretty good!

Colleagues or Competitors

One of the most valuable lessons that I've learned in my entrepreneurial career is to value my competitors. In fact, I prefer to call them colleagues, realizing that collaborative relationships are much more beneficial to everyone than cut-throat, competitive relationships based on fear and secrecy.

The reality of our world's economy is that there is plenty of business for just about any entrepreneur, as long as you're good at what you do. If that's the case, then consider all that you have to gain from working cooperatively with other businesses:

- Shared market information
- Shared industry and economic data

- Shared problem-solving competencies for issues negatively impacting your entire industry or profession
- A common business purpose and vision
- A shared sense of community

One word of warning ... do not share your intellectual property with your competitors. This would include things such as the specific ingredients for the food products that you make, the unique chemical structures of the pharmaceuticals that you manufacture, the specialized programming code you developed, and the best-in-class client-service program you've created, just to name a few. Although I strongly favor collegial relationships, do not go overboard. It is not my intention that you give all of your trade secrets away to your competitors!

Just Let It Go

Every entrepreneur experiences failure and disappointment. The successful entrepreneur, however, learns from those experiences, pulls him or herself up by the bootstraps, and keeps moving forward. My rule of thumb is that you're only allowed a day or two of moping; then it's back to business as usual—or better!

One of the hardest lessons for an entrepreneur to learn is to let it go. It can be a bad debt, an unhappy customer, a tense negotiation, a difficult transaction, disappointing sales revenues, or an unprofitable year. Of course, you're going to think about it and decide how to do it better in the future, so there's no reason to beat yourself up.

Everyone—entrepreneurs included—make mistakes and poor judgment calls. It's part of our human factor. The lesson, then, is to realize that every mistake is an opportunity to learn and discover so that you don't make those same mistakes and errors in judgment in the future. Sit back and let yourself off the hook! If you don't, you'll make yourself crazy and then who will run your business?

Lifestyle Management and Self-Care

The most valuable asset that your business has is you! Whether you're still in the start-up stages of your entrepreneurial venture or have been in business for years, most likely everything revolves around you, your skills, your capabilities, your contacts, and more. As such, it is imperative that you learn to protect that asset by taking impeccable care of it.

That's where the dilemma arises. Most entrepreneurs work well in excess of 40 hours a week, often work very long days and well into night, have an intense number of demands to deal with on a daily basis, and frankly, have little time left over to take care of themselves. There is always something more pressing to be taken care of, another deadline to be met, another customer to follow up with, or another fire to put out.

In fact, many entrepreneurs frequently ask themselves:

- Where did my personal life go?
- Where is my mental health and how can I get it back?

These are not easy questions to answer and, in fact, the answers are different for everyone. Your challenge is to identify what it is that renews you, reminds you of who you are, and allows you to balance all your work time with some personal time. For some of us, a day at the spa is intensely invigorating and renewing—for both our body and our mind. For others, a day alone with our thoughts, our pets, and a great book is all that it takes. For some of my colleagues, it's a day out on the boat, a day of shopping, a great movie, a new toolbox (with matching tools!), or an evening at home with friends and family. Whatever works for you is the right answer!

Other essential self-care items for the entrepreneur include:

- Nutritious meals and snacks
- Vitamin supplements (for the meals that you're going to inevitably miss!)
- Enough sleep to survive
- Frequent exercise (even if only for a few minutes)
- Annual medical exams

Family time and family commitments can also present difficult situations for an entrepreneur. How do you say no to your five-year-old who is begging for an afternoon with Dad when you promised to finalize that sales contract? What do you say to your 18-year-old daughter when you promised to shop with her for a prom dress, but there's been a robbery at your convenience store?

Again, these are not simple questions to answer and you'll most likely find yourself always searching for that infamous life balance that is so very difficult to capture. Your family needs you and expects to be able to spend time with you. It doesn't matter that you can rationalize to yourself that you're really working for them, not just for yourself. You can tell yourself over and over that the money you earn will pay for your child's college education, for that beautiful home, for a new car, and so much more. At some point, those concepts become vague and all that matters is that you're around and accessible to your family and your friends.

Here are a few strategies that might help you find family time without having to forfeit time away from your business:

- Pick one night each week that is family dinner night—no matter what!

- Schedule an hour or two each week to spend alone with each of your children for that special time.

- Make time to attend your child's sporting events, recitals, or other public appearances as often as is possible.

- Schedule a date once a month for an evening out with your spouse, life partner, or significant other.

- In cooperation with your family, schedule each year's vacation well in advance so that you can have the better part of the year to plan, discuss, and coordinate your trip.

Finding work/life balance—or blend—is critical to your long-term entrepreneurial success. Don't let yourself forget this!

Growth: What Does It Look Like to You?

Consider these facts about growth:

- Bigger does not necessarily mean better or more profitable.

- More staff does not necessarily mean better or more profitable.

- Increased number of customers does not necessarily mean better or more profitable.

- Larger market share does not necessarily mean better or more profitable.

- A greater variety of products does not necessarily mean better or more profitable.

- More services does not necessarily mean better or more profitable.

Get the idea? For most entrepreneurs, what does mean better is quite simple—it's being more profitable. It's all about making more money (profits) in your business and earning more money (income) for yourself. That's the primary reason why most entrepreneurs are in business. Of course, many entrepreneurs have loftier goals—to deliver one-of-a-kind products, to create new technologies, to feed the hungry, or to combat environmental destruction—and that is truly wonderful. However, when it comes right down to it, most people go into business for themselves so that they can make money, pure and simple.

Taking that one step further, the obvious conclusion is that the longer you've been in business, the more money that you want to make, should make, and can probably make. That's not the issue. Rather, the challenge is to determine how to grow your business so that you *can* make more money.

There is no magic formula for business growth, development, and expansion. What works in one industry may not work in another; what works for one solo entrepreneur may not work for another; what works in one market may not work in another. As such, you'll need to evaluate a host of business-development alternatives to determine which one(s) is most appropriate for your business and which will, most likely, prove to be the most valuable.

Of course, you'll begin by evaluating some of the more traditional strategies for growth such as:

- Hiring more staff
- Capturing more customers
- Expanding into new markets
- Developing new products
- Expanding your service portfolio

To determine which of these strategies is right for your business will require a lot of research, analysis, and number-crunching, for each will require additional resources (e.g., money, facilities, technology, engineering, material, equipment).

It's not enough to forecast what your sales revenues will be if you expand into a new consumer market. You may think that it's great that your sales are increasing and you're capturing new customers. However, that's only part of the picture. You also need to determine what that sales increase will *cost* to determine whether or not there will be a profit margin. Business growth is a step-by-step process, so be very careful that you take all of the steps—in order—to be certain you know where you're headed. To the bank with a big deposit would be great!

There are also some less-traditional strategies for business growth and expansion including:

- Franchising
- Strategic Alliances, Partnerships, and Joint Ventures
- Mergers and Acquisitions

Franchising

- **Franchise:** License granted by a company (the franchiser) to an individual or firm (franchisee) to operate a company where the franchisee agrees to use the franchiser's name; products and/or services; selling, distribution, and merchandising methods; and advertising and promotional campaigns.

If you have a business that is easily replicable and has been proven to work well operationally and perform well financially, then franchising may be a growth option that you should consider. This is a phenomenally huge initiative, but one that has the potential for tremendous financial reward. Think about McDonald's, MAACO, Minuteman Press, RE/MAX Real Estate, Play It Again Sports, Hilton Hotels, and the new, rapidly expanding Geeks on Call.

The list of successful franchises is impressive, but statistically insignificant when compared to the number of companies that attempt to franchise and fail. Preparing a business for franchising is a remarkably complex process which will cost a lot a money, consume a huge amount of time, and involve an entire team of professionals (e.g., accountants, attorneys, investors, state and federal regulatory personnel).

In theory, when you sell a franchise, you're offering individual entre-preneurs the opportunity to purchase a "business in a box" that is easily replicable and comes with complete instructions and support for set-up and long-term, profitable operation. In theory, it sounds great! However, you—as the franchiser—cannot be responsible for the skills, competencies, and performance of your individual franchisees.

If everyone who purchased your franchise did a great job, operated in strict accordance with the franchise contract, made money, and met their financial obligations to you, it would be a wonderful world. Unfortunately, no matter how spectacular your franchise operation is, there will be fran-chisees that simply do not perform well for a host of reasons (e.g., personal incompetence, refusal to comply with franchise requirements, inability to pay the franchiser).

In turn, you may find yourself involved in countless lawsuits brought against your company by the franchisees. I'm not saying they're valid legal actions or that individual franchisees will win their claims. The reality is, however, that their actions will cost you time and money, and can be extremely stressful. If you're really serious about franchising, you need to ask yourself if you're going to be able to deal with the legal issues that every successful franchised company must handle.

The most important step in franchising is knowledge. As such, I strongly recommend you consult one or more of the following resources so that you can begin to build your knowledge base and better understand the complex, intriguing, and potentially high-yield world of corporate franchising.

- **Fran Docs**   *www.frandocs.com*
- **Franchise Times Magazine**   *www.franchisetimes.com*
- **Franchise-Update**   *www.franchise-update.com*
- **Franchise Works**   *www.franchiseworks.com*
- **FranNet**   *www.frannet.com*
- **iFranchise Group**   *www.ifranchise.net*
- **International Franchise Association**   *www.franchise.org*
- **McGrow Consulting**   *www.mcgrow.com*

I also strongly urge you to consult the Federal Trade Commission's and the Small Business Association's websites to obtain critical regulatory, legal, and licensing information for potential franchisers:

- *www.ftc.gov/bcp/menu-fran.htm*
- *www.sba.gov/hotlist/franchise.html*

Acquisitions, Joint Ventures, Mergers, and Partnerships

- **Acquisition:** One company purchasing or taking over controlling interest in another company.
- **Merger:** Combination of two or more companies into one entity.
- **Joint Venture:** Agreement between two or more parties to work together on one specific project.

- **Partnership:** Agreement between two or more parties to work together on many projects.

It may be that at some point along your entrepreneurial path, you may want to investigate external strategies for growth. In the earlier part of this section, we discussed internal capabilities for growth (e.g., new products, new services, new markets, increased staffing). If you've already addressed your internal capabilities and are now ready to look outward for growth opportunities, acquisitions, joint ventures, mergers, and/or partnerships may be avenues you'll want to consider.

Although these types of business transactions vary widely, they all share one common denominator that is critically important to most entrepreneurs —letting go of some of the control of your business. When you enter into an arrangement with another person or another company, you have instantly put yourself in a position of shared responsibility for planning, operations, decision making, and more. No longer are you in total control. Instead, depending on your specific arrangement, you'll need to consult with business partners, co-owners, and others as you move your business into its next stage of growth.

Each of these transactions has its plusses and its minuses. Some may be right for you and your business; others will not. As you begin to explore these opportunities, your first step should be extensive research into how these business arrangements are formed, what is required of each participant, who will manage what specific operations and functions, how the financial aspects of the business will be managed, and how each owner/partner will be paid. This is just a sampling of the hundreds of questions you'll need to investigate to determine (1) if these types of arrangements are appropriate for you, and (2) which one of the four is the best option considering your specific business, personal, and entrepreneurial objectives.

When I did an Internet search for acquisitions, joint ventures, mergers, and business partnerships, there were thousands of websites that appeared. Most of these sites are for-profit companies interested in providing legal, financial, operating, and management-consulting expertise to individuals and companies interested in such transactions. My recommendation is that you spend some time reading about all of these companies, what services they offer, what free information you can obtain, and more as your first step in exploring these opportunities. Here are just a few to get you started:

- *http://business.library.emory.edu/info/mergers_and_acquisitions/index.html*

- *http://investopedia.com/university/mergers/*
- *http://partneringagreements.com/31jv.htm?c1=ppc&source= goo1&kw=joint-ventures*
- *http://www.1000ventures.com/business_guide/jv_main.html*
- *www.BeyondTheArc.com*
- *www.business.com/directory/financial_services/investment_banking_ and_brokerage/mergers_and_acquisitions_manda/*
- *www.imergersacquisitions.com/*
- *http://www.law.cornell.edu/wex/index.php/Joint_venture*
- *www.masource.org*
- *www.valuationresources.com*

Business Etiquette and Protocol for the Successful Entrepreneur

Remember the days of white kid gloves, women in dresses (never in slacks!), and men in evening jackets and ascots? In generations past, etiquette and protocol were critically important in both your personal and your professional life.

My, how things have changed! What hasn't changed, however, is the fact that there are still established rules for etiquette and protocol that, despite the often familiar and casual tone of today's business world, are quite important. I recommend that you review the following information closely to be certain that you're up to par on today's acceptable business protocols.

Note that this information is excerpted from "Lessons in Etiquette," a collection of articles written by Margaret Develey, an expert in corporate etiquette and political protocol. For more information on Margaret Develey, visit *www.develeyintl.com.*

Business Entertaining

- When you invite a client or business associate to a meal, you should select the restaurant and be very specific about the time and place you will meet.
- If you're meeting at the table, do not order anything before your guest arrives—not even water—and leave the napkins untouched. Your guest needs to see a perfectly set table.

- Sit your guest across from you or to your right (the position designated for the guest of honor).

- When you order, let your guest order first, but give some guidance such as "The food here is excellent. I have always enjoyed the filet mignon and lobster salad." Or, "They have some excellent wines here." This will set the "limits" of your hospitality.

- Your meal should be comparable to that of your guest. If your guest orders an appetizer, entree, and dessert, order the same. You do not, however, need to order an alcoholic beverage even if your guest does. A mineral water with a twist will do.

- If you need to open papers for your business discussion, wait until the meal is over and the entree plates have been removed.

- The guest should always send a handwritten thank-you note to the host within 24 hours.

Dining Etiquette

- Wait for your host or hostess to place their napkin on their lap, thus indicating the beginning of a meal, before you place yours on your lap.

- Wait for the host or hostess to start drinking before you do so, even if it is water.

- Your solid food items (e.g., bread) should always be on your left and the liquids (e.g., coffee) always on your right.

- Do not butter your bread in the air. Cut a small piece in your plate and butter it there.

- Keep both elbows close to your body when cutting food.

- Sunglasses, car keys, cell phones, day-timers, and handbags have no place on a dining table.

- Cell phones and pagers should be turned off while dining.

- Lipstick and toothpicks are to be used away from the table.

- Stem glasses are to be held by the stem.

- Napkins are to be left on the chair if you leave your seat temporarily and on the left of your place setting when you are finished.

Meeting Etiquette

- Never schedule a meeting on a Friday afternoon or the day before a major holiday.

- Always distribute an agenda ahead of time so people can prepare. Bring extra copies of the agenda with you to the meeting (electronic copy if you're having a virtual meeting).

- Start and finish your meeting on time. This shows your respect for the participants and consideration for their time.

- If you're attending a meeting, do not sit until someone indicates where you should sit and never sit to the immediate right or immediate left of the chairperson. Those seats are reserved for the "honored" guests and peers.

- Introduce yourself to others in the room if there is no one there to introduce you. Be sure to hand out your business cards and collect others. When seated, place the business cards you've collected in front of you so that you can remember the names of the people you met.

- When wearing a name badge, always place it on the right. The eyes of the person you are addressing will go to the side of your extended hand first.

- When attending a business function, always keep your right hand free for handshaking.

At the End...

Whether it's today, tomorrow, next year, or 20 years from now, there may come a day when you make the decision that it's time to move on and leave your entrepreneurial career behind. You want to cash out, take your money, and move on with your life.

This is a huge decision for most entrepreneurs. For some, the decision is based on negative factors. They've had enough of the constant demands on them and their time, they haven't enjoyed the financial rewards they had anticipated, or their business has simply never taken off and done well. At that point, many entrepreneurs simply give up and move on.

If you fall into this category of entrepreneurs who have reached the end, our hope is that you've reaped some rewards from your experience. This might include new skills and talents you've acquired that will make you more marketable in the workplace, new contacts that you've made that will prove fruitful, new technologies that you've mastered, new professions and industries you've been exposed to, and so much more. Every experience —even if you consider it a failure—always provides us with tools for our future. I can guarantee that your entrepreneurial experience will do the same for you!

Fortunately, many other entrepreneurs make the decision to transition out of their businesses for very positive reasons:

- They can close their businesses, take all of the money they've earned, and retire.

- They can close their businesses, take all of the money they've earned, and transition back into the workforce.

- They can sell their businesses for a nice return on their years of hard work and investment.

- They have positioned their businesses as prime candidates to be acquired by other, larger companies.

- They have decided to hand over the daily management of their companies to another individual (e.g., business partner, relative, protégé), removing themselves from the day-to-day operations while still retaining some percentage of ownership interest.

If you've reached this point in your entrepreneurial career, let me first congratulate you! As you read in Chapter 1, *Welcome to the World of Entrepreneurship,* the odds were against you and statistics predicted your failure, yet you succeeded. You should take tremendous pride and satisfaction in what you have accomplished and realize that you're definitely one of the chosen few who've made it this far.

I have sold four small businesses over the course of my entrepreneurial career—one in 1988, one in 1994, one in 1999, and the last one in 2004. Even though all four of these businesses were profitable, I knew that it was time for me to move on and change my own career direction. I refer to it as the *entrepreneur's disease*—I get bored once everything is up and running profitably, and need to find new challenges and new opportunities.

In three situations, I sold my businesses to employees who had worked for me for years. In the fourth situation, I sold to one of my Board members. Obviously, each of these individuals knew the business well, how it operated, what was involved, what resources were necessary, what the customers expected, and much more. In turn, it made all four of these sales and ownership transitions relatively easy and seamless.

There are certain distinct advantages and disadvantages to selling in this manner:

- The actual selling process and ownership transition is relatively easy and seamless.

- The sale happens much faster than if you worked with a business broker, placed advertisements, and otherwise attempted to sell your business.

- You may have to extend credit to your buyer and hold a promissory note for the bulk of payment to be paid out over time (usually years).

- The selling price of your business may be lower than if you were to sell it on the open market.

Whatever decisions you make—about how to move away from your business and what career path you want to pursue now—will require a great deal of personal introspection. It is not a decision that should be made lightly, nor should it be made when things are not going particularly well with your business. If that's the case, you may find yourself making a decision out of desperation and that's a terrible strategy for any major life change. Rather, you want to make your decision from a position of power and success.

I'm a die-hard entrepreneur and would never consider any other path. I know that it's my destiny to work for myself and I realize how tremendously fortunate I am to be able to make a good living. So few people in today's working world have the luxury of doing what they love, each and every day of their lives. So few people have the degree of control that I have—to determine what I want to do, how I want to do it, and when I want to do it. Of course there are ups and downs as with everything else in anyone's life. Yet I know that I'm truly blessed in the decisions I've made and in my entrepreneurial self.

I hope that everyone reading this book will enjoy the good fortune that I've enjoyed, realizing that it takes a tremendous amount of hard work and effort. If you have true entrepreneurial spirit and drive, it will lead you in the right direction and afford you all of the opportunities awaiting each and every one of you.

May the entrepreneurial heavens shine down on you, and may you enjoy professional and personal fulfillment every day of your life!

Subject Index

A

Accounting, 118, 150
Acquisitions, 200
Advertising, 58, 75-76
Assessment, 11, 15-19
Automating, 176

B

Blogs, 158
Board of directors, 55
Boredom, ii, 204
Brand:
    defining, 58
    identifying unique, 67-69
    image, 66
    loyalty, 66
    name, 70
Branding, 65-71
Business:
    buying, 32
    cards, 74
    customer-centric, 37-38
    development, 58-60
    economic-centric, 38-39
    etiquette, 201-203
    family-owned, 37
    growth, 184-205
    model, 20-21, 37-41
    name, 43
    options, 31-37
    plan, 28-56
    selling, 203-205
    service-centric, 39-41
    type, 29-31
Businesses:
    defining, 14, 19-20
    failed, 10
    number of, 1
    options, 14, 19-20
    small, 1
    trends, 11

C

Coaches, 191-193
Clients, 85-109, 107
Colleagues, 193-194
Collections, 128-130
Competencies, 4-6
Competitors, 193-194
Consistency, 59
Corporation, 48
Credit, 129

Credit cards, 124, 126, 149-150
Customer:
   care, 60, 85-109
   relationship management, 86-87
   retention, 103-107
   satisfaction, 103-107
   service, 102-103
   types, 72
Customers, 85-109

D

Database management, 150
Deadlines, 176
Delivery, 102
Direct-sales, 19, 33-34
Dreams, 1
Drive, 12

E

E-commerce tools, 154-158
Email, 150-154
Entertaining, 201-202
Entrepreneurial:
   competencies, 17-19
   cycles, 190
   drive, 15-16
   lifestyle, 189-196
   options, 31-37
   pitfalls, 23-24
   resources, 24-27
   self-care, 195-196
   skills, 17-19
   success, 5, 42
   team, 22-23
Entrepreneurs:
   American, 9-10
   opportunities for, ii
   sole, 191
   successful, 11-14
Entrepreneurship:
   benefits of, 2
   realities, 2
   trends in, 1
   truth about, ii
Equipment requirements, 54
Equity interest, 36-37
Etiquette, 201-203
Executive summary, 46-47
Expectations:
   exceeding, 103
   realistic, ii
Expenses, 121-122

F

Failure, 10
Finance, 115-117

Financial:
   management, 110-133
   plan, 51-52
Franchises, 20, 34-36
Franchising, 198-199

G

Goals, 7

H

Human resources (see Staffing)

I

Image, 66
Income:
   creating, 117-128
   passive, 127
Index cards, 178
Internet, 99
IRS, 130-131

J

Joint ventures, 199

L

Legal business structure, 47-49
Lessons learned, i
Licenses, 50
Likability, 59, 93
Lists, 178
LLC, 48

M

Management:
   corporate, 139-140
   lifestyle, 143-145, 194-196
   materials, 138
   pile, 168-170
   quality, 139
   time, 168-173
Market:
   mix, 62
   plan, 62
   research, 61
   segmentation, 61
   share, 61
   test, 61-62
Marketing, 57-84
Marketing plan, 53-54
Materials, 52, 138-139
Mergers, 199
Mission statement 43-45
Mistakes, I
Money, 110-133
Motivation, 3-4, 7-8

Multi-level marketing, 33
Multi-tasking, 12

N

Networking:
  interpersonal, 8, 61,
    99-100, 132
  online, 159-160
Newsletters, 63-65

O

Operating plan, 50
Operations:
  business, 51, 134-145
  manual, 136
Opportunities, 10-11

P

Partnerships, 200
Patrons, 85-109
Permits, 50
Personal relationships, 59-60
Personnel, 55-56
Planning, 141-143
Policy and procedures, 135-136
Press relations, 76-77
Press releases, 76-84
Pricing, 122-125
Prioritizing, 176
Problem-solving, 140-141, 187-189
Productivity, 167-183
Professional:
  assistance, 132
  associations, 100
Promotions, 58
Proprietorship, 49
Public relations, 58, 76-77
Purchasing, 138-139

R

Referrals, 73
Regulatory requirements, 50
Research:
  businesses, 8
  importance of, 21-22
Resources:
  business development, 76-78
  business plan, 56-57
  customer relationship
    management, 107-109
  entrepreneurial, 24-27
  franchising, 199
  marketing, 77-78
  productivity, 182-183
  sales, 77-78
  technology, 164-165

  time management, 182-183
  veterans, 27
Retirement plan, 128
Rewards, 3
Risks:
  managing, 8-9
  taking, 2, 12

S

Sales
  connections, 71-72
  defining, 59
  invisible, 72
  person-to-person, 68
  plan, 53
  telephone, 72
  tips, 73-75
Skills, 4
Software, 148-149
Spam, 160, 162
Staffing, 50, 136-138
Success, 184-205

T

Taxes, 130-131
Technology:
  requirements, 54
  toolkit, 147-162
  use of, 146-165
Terminology, 58-60, 111-115
Thank-you notes, 95
Time:
  management, 167-184
  wasters, 171-173
Trademark, 70
Troublesome clients, 107

U

Uncertainty, 13

V

Virtual assistant, 161-164
Viruses, 160-161
Vision statement, 43-46
Voice-mail, 94

W

Websites, 154-158
Work/life balance, 143-145

Resource Index

Self-Assessments

Entrepreneurial Drive and Spirit, 15-16
Entrepreneurial Skills and Competencies,
   17-19

Planning Worksheets

Business Plan Tools, Resources,
   and Templates, 56
Daily Task Management, 178
Identifying Your Unique Brand, 69-71
Monthly Budget, 123
Monthly Task Management, 180
Weekly Task Management, 179
Your Entrepreneurial Decisions, 40

Useful Internet Resources

Acquisitions, joint ventures, mergers, and
   partnerships, 200
Anti-virus programs, 161
Blogs, 158
Bookkeeping/accounting, 149
Branding, 67
Business start-up, 26-27
Coaches, 190
Credit card merchant, 126

Customer relationship management, 109
Database management, 150
Direct sales, 33
E-commerce, 155
Email accounts, 151
Email broadcasting, 154
Financial concepts, 111-115
Firewalls, 161-162
Franchising, 35-36, 199
Newsletters, 64
Online networking, 159
Operating manuals, 136
Sales, marketing, and
   business development, 78
Spam filters, 162
Start-up financing, 115
Tax resources, 130-131
Technology tools, 147-148, 165
Time management, 182
Veterans assistance, 27
Virtual assistants, 164
Website templates, 156-158

Entrepreneurship and Career Resources

THE FOLLOWING RESOURCES are available directly from Impact Publications. Full descriptions of each title as well as downloadable catalogs, videos, software, games, posters, and related products can be found on our website: www.impact publications.com. Complete this form or list the titles, include shipping (see formula at the end), enclose payment, and send your order to:

IMPACT PUBLICATIONS
9104 Manassas Drive, Suite N
Manassas Park, VA 20111-5211 USA
1-800-361-1055 (orders only)
Tel. 703-361-7300 or Fax 703-335-9486
Email address: query@impactpublications.com
Quick & easy online ordering: *www.impactpublications.com*

Orders from individuals must be prepaid by check, money order, or major credit card. We accept telephone, fax, and email orders.

Qty.	TITLES	Price	TOTAL
Entrepreneurship			
____	101 Small Business Ideas for Under $5,000	$19.95	_____
____	201 Great Ideas for Your Small Business	19.95	_____
____	202 Things You Can Buy and Sell for Big Profits!	19.95	_____
____	The $100,000+ Entrepreneur	19.95	_____
____	Business Plans Kit for Dummies (with CD-ROM)	34.99	_____

_____ Complete Idiot's Guide to Starting a
         Home-Based Business   18.95 _____
_____ How to Buy, Sell, and Profit on eBay   13.95 _____
_____ Home-Based Business for Dummies   19.99 _____
_____ The Martha Rules   15.95 _____
_____ McGraw-Hill Guide to Starting Your Own Business   14.95 _____
_____ Six-Week Start-Up   19.95 _____
_____ Small Business for Dummies   21.99 _____
_____ Small Business Owner's Manual   19.99 _____
_____ Small Business Marketing for Dummies   19.99 _____
_____ The Small Business Start-Up Kit   24.99 _____
_____ Start Your Own Business   24.95 _____
_____ The Successful Business Plan   29.95 _____
_____ What Business Should I Start?   19.95 _____
_____ What No One Ever Tells You About Starting
         Your Own Business   18.95 _____

Attitude and Motivation

_____ 100 Ways to Motivate Yourself   14.99 _____
_____ Attitude Is Everything   14.95 _____
_____ Awaken the Giant Within   16.00 _____
_____ Change Your Attitude   15.99 _____
_____ Change Your Thinking, Change Your Life   16.95 _____
_____ Eat That Frog!   15.95 _____
_____ Goals!   15.95 _____
_____ Little Gold Book of YES! Attitude   19.99 _____
_____ Success Principles   15.95 _____

Inspiration and Empowerment

_____ 7 Habits of Highly Effective People   15.95 _____
_____ The 8th Habit   15.00 _____
_____ 101 Secrets of Highly Effective Speakers   15.95 _____
_____ Create Your Own Future   16.95 _____
_____ Dream It, Do It   16.95 _____
_____ The Habit Change Workbook   19.95 _____
_____ Life Strategies   13.95 _____
_____ The Magic of Thinking Big   14.00 _____
_____ The Power of Positive Thinking (3 books in 1)   13.99 _____
_____ The Secret   23.95 _____
_____ Shine   15.95 _____
_____ Who Moved My Cheese?   19.95 _____
_____ Wishcraft   13.95 _____

Testing and Assessment

_____ Career Match   15.00 _____
_____ Career Tests   12.95 _____
_____ Discover What You're Best At   14.00 _____
_____ Do What You Are   18.95 _____
_____ Finding Your Perfect Work   16.95 _____
_____ I Could Do Anything If Only I Knew What It Was   16.00 _____
_____ I Want to Do Something Else,
         But I'm Not Sure What It Is   15.95 _____
_____ Now, Discover Your Strengths   30.00 _____

_____ What Should I Do With My Life?	14.95	_____
_____ What Type Am I?	14.95	_____
_____ What's Your Type of Career?	18.95	_____
_____ Who Do You Think You Are?	18.00	_____

Networking

_____ Endless Referrals	16.95	_____
_____ Fine Art of Small Talk	16.95	_____
_____ How to Work a Room	14.00	_____
_____ Little Black Book of Connections	19.95	_____
_____ Masters of Networking	16.95	_____
_____ Never Eat Alone	24.95	_____
_____ One Phone Call Away	24.95	_____
_____ Power Networking	14.95	_____
_____ The Savvy Networker	13.95	_____
_____ Work the Pond!	15.95	_____

Dress, Image, and Etiquette

_____ Business Etiquette for Dummies	21.99	_____
_____ Dressing Smart for Men	16.95	_____
_____ Dressing Smart for the New Millennium	15.95	_____
_____ Dressing Smart for Women	16.95	_____
_____ Power Etiquette	15.95	_____
_____ You've Only Got Three Seconds	15.00	_____

Interviews

_____ 101 Dynamite Questions to Ask At Your Job Interview	13.95	_____
_____ High-Impact Interview Questions	17.95	_____
_____ Haldane's Best Answers to Tough Interview Questions	15.95	_____
_____ How to Ace the Brain Teaser Interview	14.95	_____
_____ I Can't Believe They Asked Me That!	17.95	_____
_____ Job Interview Tips for People With Not-So-Hot Backgrounds	14.95	_____
_____ Job Interviews for Dummies	16.99	_____
_____ KeyWords to Nail Your Job Interview	17.95	_____
_____ Nail the Job Interview!	14.95	_____
_____ The Savvy Interviewer	10.95	_____
_____ Win the Interview, Win the Job	15.95	_____
_____ You Have 3 Minutes!	21.95	_____

Salary Negotiations

_____ Dynamite Salary Negotiations	15.95	_____
_____ Get a Raise in 7 Days	14.95	_____
_____ Negotiating Your Salary	12.95	_____
_____ Salary Negotiation Tips for Professionals	16.95	_____
_____ Secrets of Power Salary Negotiating	13.99	_____

Career Exploration and Job Strategies

_____ 50 Best Jobs for Your Personality	16.95	_____
_____ 300 Best Jobs Without a Four-Year Degree	16.95	_____
_____ About.com Guide to Job Searching	17.95	_____

_____	America's Top 100 Jobs for People Without a Four-Year Degree	19.95	_____
_____	America's Top Jobs for People Re-Entering the Workforce	19.95	_____
_____	Change Your Job, Change Your Life	21.95	_____
_____	How to Succeed Without a Career Path	13.95	_____
_____	Quit Your Job and Grow Some Hair	15.95	_____
_____	What Color Is Your Parachute?	17.95	_____

Resumes and Letters

_____	201 Dynamite Job Search Letters	19.95	_____
_____	Best KeyWords for Resumes, Cover Letters, & Interviews	17.95	_____
_____	Best Resumes and CVs for International Jobs	24.95	_____
_____	Best Resumes for $100,000+ Jobs	24.95	_____
_____	Best Resumes for People Without a Four-Year Degree	19.95	_____
_____	Best Cover Letters for $100,000+ Jobs	24.95	_____
_____	Blue Collar Resume and Job Hunting Guide	15.95	_____
_____	Haldane's Best Cover Letters for Professionals	15.95	_____
_____	Haldane's Best Resumes for Professionals	15.95	_____
_____	High Impact Resumes and Letters	19.95	_____
_____	Nail the Cover Letter!	17.95	_____
_____	Nail the Resume!	17.95	_____
_____	Resume, Application, and Letter Tips for People With Hot and Not-So-Hot Backgrounds	17.95	_____
_____	Resumes for Dummies	16.99	_____
_____	Winning Letters That Overcome Barriers to Employment	17.95	_____

SUBTOTAL
Virginia residents add 5% sales tax   _____

_____

POSTAGE/HANDLING
($5 for first product and 8% of SUBTOTAL)   _____
8% of SUBTOTAL   _____

TOTAL ENCLOSED .... _____

SHIP TO:

Name: _____

Address: _____

_____

_____

PAYMENT METHOD:

❑ I enclose check/money order for $_____ made payable to IMPACT PUBLICATIONS.

❑ Please charge $_____ to my credit card:

❑ Visa ❑ MasterCard ❑ American Express ❑ Discover

Card #_____Expiration date: ____/____

Signature _____

Keep in Touch...
On the Web!

www.impactpublications.com
www.ishoparoundtheworld.com
www.exoffenderreentry.com
www.travel-smarter.com
www.winningthejob.com
www.veteransworld.com